Putting Social Media To Work 3.0:
For The Busy Executive

Gemma Dale
@HR_Gem

Tim Scott
@TimScottHR

Cover art by **Simon Heath**
@SimonHeath1

Throughout this book we have given Twitter handles (read on if you're not sure what that means!) wherever possible for named individuals or organisations. These are shown as @username.

First edition: January 2017

From 251112 to here - so far.

Contents

Why you should care about social media.

Seth Godin described social media as the greatest shift of our generation. We tend to agree with him. We have also heard it described as the greatest shift in the workplace since the industrial revolution. We believe that it arguably offers greater opportunities to rethink some of the old ways of working than organisations, business leaders and individual professionals have ever had before.

Social media has become a ubiquitous subject. Discussions abound on how to recruit with social media, how to get your CEO to be social, how to sell socially, headlines about employees who have posted something dubious finding themselves on the receiving end of their P45, even people who are divorcing because of Facebook behaviour. But for every individual and organisation embracing it, there is another who is fearful of it, and another that just hasn't got a clue what all the fuss is about. The world has changed, is changing, is going to change some more. It has always been the case. And right at the centre of this intensifying change is technology, and social technology in particular. Driving new ways of working and communicating and creating new opportunities; for organisations and individuals alike. The old rules no longer apply. We must rethink the way we work, sell, engage, communicate, lead, talk to customers and build and manage our reputations and brands. We need to rethink leadership in this new context.

We live in an increasingly open and transparent world. Many of us think nothing now of putting our entire CV online for people to view. Tweeting our everyday lives, and sharing our thoughts with the world. Or our followers at least. There is no home time/work time dividing line, just more and more blurred lines. For good or for bad, we are constantly connected. Always on. Anywhere and any when. In the office or the **Coffice**.

For organisations and their leaders, there is an important and simple truth of the new social world. Your customers are there. Your employees are there. Your competitors are too. People are talking about your brand online, whether you like it or not. They might be talking about you too. There is a saying in the social media world; the conversation is happening anyway so you might as well be part of it. Resisting this truth is akin to denying the existence of the telephone.

Social has the power to change everything; it is that impactful. How we communicate and collaborate at a fundamental level. How we sell and market our services. How we lead and how we learn. How we engage and communicate with the people that work for us and the people that buy from us. How we actually do the day job. Who has the power? Who is considered to be a leader (and in the social world that might mean someone other than the one with the executive title). Where we physically sit to do the work that we do. No longer are we limited to or by our immediate team, organisation, locality, time zone.

For all of these reasons, and many more besides, being able to use social media as a leader is becoming increasingly important. And by this, we don't mean having a LinkedIn profile that you never update. This isn't being active on social media by any definition.

In this little book, we are going to aim to do a few things. Firstly, explain why understanding social and being social is so important for leaders and organisations alike, and why, whatever your personal view on all things social, you cannot ignore it. We are going to share own experiences about what social has done for us and other stories from those who have successfully used social media as part of their leadership toolkit. And then we will give you some ideas about how you can get started and some key rules to follow.

This book isn't specifically about social media for your organisation. We've written about that too (shameless plug for our other books alert). This book is about why **you**, as a leader of an organisation, need to get out there on social media and how to do it. Of course, to reap the benefits of being a social leader, you need a social organisation too. So we will include some thoughts on this along the way – about how to take your people with you on the journey.

We recognise that people will come to this book with varying levels of knowledge about social media and technology – from ninja to newbie.

As you go through the book, you'll come across some more technical words and/or jargon terms that are highlighted in **bold**. This means they are explained in a bit more detail in the Glossary at the back.

Are you sitting comfortably? Because we're about to enter the social world.

What the heck is social media anyway?

When a lot of people hear the term social media, their first thought is of networks like Facebook or Twitter. They think about the social side of social media. But social media is much, much more than that.

At its most basic level, social media is about any platform or application that allows you to share content with other people, sometimes publicly and sometimes to a prescribed audience chosen by you, and that allow you to participate in networking activity. It takes many forms.

It does include those social applications we have already mentioned.

It also includes **blogs** and **vlogs** like **Tumblr** and **WordPress**.

It includes content communities like **YouTube**.

It includes professional networking like **LinkedIn**.

It includes messaging and photo apps like **Snapchat** and Instagram.

It includes community sites like **Google+** and apps designed for team work such as **Slack**.

It includes forums and virtual gaming.

It includes live video broadcasting like **Periscope** and Facebook Live.

It includes collaborative projects (often called "**crowdsourced**") like Wikipedia.

Social media is online technology that enables the sharing of ideas and information, and allows comment and discussion and debate, whether on a tablet or a PC or a mobile.

There are two very important facts that you need to know about social media. Firstly, it is a world that is constantly evolving. Any list of social media applications and platforms would be out of date the moment it was written. And secondly, its use is increasing exponentially, including across all generations.

Facts and Figures

Figures sourced from the United Nations show that the number of people using the internet has now reached 3.4 billion. We are approaching the point where 50% of the planet's population are using the internet. Nearly a third are using social media. Yes, you did read that correctly.

At the same time, traditional methods of communication like email, **snail mail** and the phone have declined. Fewer people have a home landline. Some organisations are going entirely email free. Others are only accepting job applications via Twitter.

These numbers get out of date as soon as they are printed, but at the time of writing, 73% of UK adults use the internet daily, and 50% of them are using social networking sites. Internet users have an average of over five social media accounts. Every second, there are 12 new social media users added.

Facebook has 1.7 billion users, 23% of whom access the site more than five times a day. Facebook and WhatsApp handle between them 60 million messages every single day.

LinkedIn now has 300 million members. **Pinterest** has 100 million members. 500 million tweets are sent every day by over 320 million users. There are over 300 million micro blogs on **Tumblr**. 110 million more post their photos over at **Instagram**. And **YouTube** has over 1 billion users worldwide.

Four out of five purchases are influenced by online content. Over 80% of businesses saying that they research and find suppliers online.

By 2025, 5 billion people will be connected by mobile devices.

Part of this extraordinary growth in internet use is based on the smart phone, something 53% of us now carry around in our pockets. A tipping point has been reached and breached with now more than half of internet connections made via a mobile device. Except for **LinkedIn** - which remains mostly desktop - all of the main social media sites are accessed primarily via a mobile device.

When it comes to using social media, surveys vary. But what we do know for certain is that it is not just something for younger people. Profiles of sites vary too of course: Snapchat attracts a much younger user base, whereas over on Twitter their fastest growing demographic is the 55-64 age bracket.

Remember the days when you had to sit at your computer and use a dial-up modem, with its characteristic screeching bleeping sound to access the internet? Broadband used to be a nice to have, luxury item. Now it is a life essential to most. **Cognitive Assistants** are now in our own homes through the likes of Amazon Echo. Even our domestic appliances can now be controlled from our phones and tablets. **Wearable** technology is going mainstream. Low cost **cloud computing** widely available. Phones are no longer just phones; they are **converged devices**.

As is commonly quoted, there is more computer power in your washing machine than it took to send a man to the moon. By 2020 it is estimated that computers will have the power of the human brain. If it isn't already, pretty soon your washing machine will be connected to the internet too as part of what is being called the "**Internet of things**" – in other words, the internet will become integral to many day to day activities that currently don't involve computers at all.

We are all social now. This isn't about one particular platform or social network. It is about completely new ways of working, selling, communicating. A potential promise of something better, perhaps.

Even more about different types of social stuff

We have written this chapter especially for social media newbies. It's an overview of the main platforms and types of all things social.

The most important thing to note is that this chapter will be out of date almost as soon as we have written it. There is new stuff coming along all the time; we've only mentioned the main ones or this chapter would be longer than the rest of the book combined. You can't do them all, so don't even try.

Twitter

Our favourite platform. We actually met on Twitter, and organised most of this book through its private messaging function, the handy 'DM' (which stands for direct message). The second biggest social media platform out there.

Twitter is built about one simple premise: you can only post messages made up of fewer than 140 characters. You'd probably be surprised by what you can achieve within that limit: it's possible to share images, videos, links and just straightforward comments. Out of all the platforms, you will find more of a blurring of the professional and the personal here. Twitter is great for people, great for brands, and especially great for leaders.

Blogging

We are both bloggers and we are passionate advocates of it. Blogging is basically self-publishing. No longer is **content** the preserve of journalists or paid academics. With over 60 million **WordPress** blogs, people are out there, putting their thoughts and ideas into the world for others to see. Blogging is a disruptive technology, in a good way.

Blogs are a rich stream of learning. They offer a stream of ideas straight to your computer screen, tablet or pocket. Reading them is a great way to engage with some brilliant thinking - all for free. The other power of blogs is their interactivity. People leave comments and engage with the blogger and his or her content. Blogs are generally more reflective pieces than the short snappy stuff you get on Twitter. They are also a bit more personal than the more formal business articles found on somewhere like **LinkedIn**.

There are people blogging on pretty much everything. From leadership to fitness, from fashion to music. People blog about their mental health, their politics, their favourite recipes. Work, personal, and everything in between. We'd love you to read our blogs. We think they are brilliant. But if thoughts about the worlds of work and Human Resources are not your cup of tea, then you will surely find something that works for you.

Whilst we love blogging, it is undoubtedly one of the more time-consuming of social activities in terms of content creation and maintenance. We think it is worth it though! Later on, we will talk a little more about why as a leader, you might want to consider blogging out your thoughts.

LinkedIn

The professional networking site. Think of it like your online CV, your career or business elevator pitch. It is a professional networking site, although some people still seem to get it confused with Facebook. For us, it is one of those sites that you kind of need to be on, rather than anything you can get really passionate about. We don't like the user experience all that much – there is a little too much selling and bragging for us. More and more of what used to be free on the site you now have to pay for. If it wasn't so ubiquitous, we would probably suggest going somewhere less boring instead.

These niggles aside, it does have its positives too. Having a strong profile is undoubtedly good for your personal brand as it allows you to showcase your achievements, look for work and be found by people who are recruiting. But for chat, for groups, for building relationships, we prefer other places. However, as we will say repeatedly, it is about picking what is right for you and your business, so don't let us put you off with our personal preferences.

Google+ (or G+)

Good for **Search Engine Optimisation**, which means if you want your stuff to appear high up on a Google search it is good to have your content there. If you are local business it's important to have a G+ account, as it allows you to put a pin in Google maps showing your location. You also need a G+ account to create a YouTube channel.

Pinterest

Think of it like an online notice board: a place for pinning images, videos and links onto your own noticeboards, which can be public or private. You will find everything on there from recipes, wedding ideas, fitness inspiration and motivational quotes. It's definitely growing as a platform, and can have a corporate angle too.

Instagram

It's all about sharing of pictures and video. You can follow and be followed, and can have an open account or keep it private. You can comment on other people's stuff too, as well as stalk - sorry, we mean *follow* - celebrities. You can link it up across all your other social media accounts so that your photos are uploaded to them all. It is at least partially responsible for the rise of the selfie. The best bit about it of all is that you can apply filters and all sorts of effects to your pictures, making sure that you look as good as you can before you unleash your latest photographic masterpiece on an unsuspecting world.

Facebook

The one everyone knows about. Used to be cool, now perhaps less so. It has been slightly abandoned by younger folks as their parents and grandparents get on there. We won't say much more about Facebook, because we reckon if you don't know what it is you must have been sleeping under a rock. Just one thing to note – as well as the personal profile (remember to check your privacy settings please for those concerned with their personal brand!) you can do business on here too. If you are a local business, or in the business to consumer market then you might want to think about a business page. But under no circumstances should you mix the two.

Also just released into the wild is what was being known as Facebook at Work, but has been re-christened "Workplace by Facebook" (although it's the same thing) - an internal social network for colleagues within a corporate network that looks and feels like Facebook.

Periscope

An app that is owned by Twitter and allows you to live stream video over the internet. It includes an option to make videos entirely public or just available to selected viewers. Because of the link with Twitter it also allows users to tweet a link to their video content. It is particularly useful for sharing content from events and conferences. It remains to be seen how it will be affected by Facebook's alternative, Facebook Live.

Snapchat

This one is a messaging app. Users can take pictures or videos and add text or drawings to them, then share them with their friends. The user decides how long the 'snaps' are available for – but it's usually just a few seconds, which limits its business application a little – but there are still brands out there making the most of it. It has quite a young user demographic – the **selfie** is a very popular on Snapchat. Accounts can be public or private. It's still a niche site for now.

WhatsApp

Essentially a messaging tool – globally the most popular in 2015 with 600 million active users. It is now owned by Facebook – which has got some people worried about privacy and what Facebook will do with all of that information... You can send messages between individuals and groups of people, including pictures and links. It also allows sharing of pictures and links. It used to require a small annual subscription fee but this has now been removed – and as a result it is becoming very widely used in both business and personal applications.

YouTube

Some people don't really think of YouTube as a social network. But it is about sharing content (of the video variety) and allowing people to comment on it. Thousands and thousands of hours of video footage is uploaded to YouTube every day. It is now one of the biggest search engines in the World. You will find a whole range of stuff here - TV clips, **Vlogs**, "how to" videos created by people in their garages, corporate content, music videos. If it can be filmed it will be on there. And we will leave the rest of that to your imagination.

Slack

A cross between a social media platform and an old-style internet message board. It's basically a project management-type app that is allegedly used by NASA. It allows you to get a team together in one digital place, run different conversation threads, share documents and the like. It encourages quick and easy internal collaboration.

There are many more social media platforms than just these few described here; we have simply picked a few of the biggest ones. Some are more about producing and sharing content, some more about chatting. Any book that tried to cover them all would be out of date very quickly – probably before it was printed. You can never be on every platform, there are simply too many. Our advice is just take a look, play around, and find one or two platforms that work for you and your business, and in particular where your customers are likely to be.

In a later chapter we will explore a bit more about which ones might work for you and share some top tips for getting started on the platform.

What's in it for you?

So what can social media do on a personal level for you as a leader of an organisation?

Anyone who runs their own business or holds a senior management position already has significant demands on their time and energy. So this social media stuff might just seem like one more chore on the never-ending to-do list.

But failing to engage with social media might just mean that you miss out very real opportunities. Opportunities to build your personal brand. Opportunities to engage with employees and customers alike. An opportunity to put yourself out there as an expert, or maybe find other people or businesses to collaborate with. But most of all, the opportunity to shape your organisation's culture. To challenge those common organisational ills such as silo working, communication difficulties and barriers to effective collaboration. An opportunity to reach beyond the boundaries of geography and engage directly with, and listen to, those people that work for you.

Engaging socially takes time and effort. But the benefits, both personally and organisationally, can be significant.

For us, it comes down to four broad areas from which the leader can benefit.

- Connecting

- Learning

- Personal brand

- Listening

Connecting

Let's face it: if you lead a business of any substantial size you can't get "face time" (as opposed to FaceTime!) with most of the people that work for you. Certainly for the global leader, time zones and geography get in the way. Social media can help to overcome this challenge.

It can connect you outside of your organisation too. To other leaders, to ideas, to customers, to broader ideas and new thinking. It can help you develop a personal learning network. Speaking of which......

Learning

Social media is a constant stream of ideas; new things, blogs, podcasts, tweets, video. Straight to the device in your pocket. There for you to consume when it suits you. No longer do you have to go on a training course, sit from nine until five and dutifully watch all of the PowerPoint slides. And if you follow and connect with the right people you don't even have to go looking for it, it will come to you. We love blogs for learning. 500 or so words, easy to consume, something for everyone. The truth is, whatever business you run, whatever professional you are in, you need to keep up to date and relevant to your market and your customers. Just because you have reached the top of the executive tree doesn't mean you are done learning and growing. Social just makes this easy to do. And then you can share that learning with your customers and connections. Often, especially within smaller organisations, there isn't lots of money or time available for formal courses and the like. But there is plenty of learning available in the social world. It is all out there, and a whole heck of a lot of it is free.

Personal Brand

If you want to develop your personal brand as a leader, then social media is a pretty awesome way to doing it. We know plenty of self-employed professionals who build their business around social media. Their blogs, Twitter feeds and LinkedIn profiles are a showcase for their work, as well as pretty much all of their advertising and networking activity too. Social gives you the opportunity to differentiate yourself from everyone else, put yourself out there as a bit of a "thought leader", to coin an overused phrase. It is an old saying that people buy from people. But there is truth to be found in clichés. Having a face to your brand can be a big influencer in purchasing decisions. It is much more personal than a company website can ever be. Some leaders have been very successful in developing their organisation's brand by promoting their own management philosophies – maybe you could be the next?

Listening

Want to have direct access to the latest thinking on business leadership in general or in your particular sector? Want to know what your customers or target customers are talking about? Or the people that work for you? What they are thinking and feeling? And most importantly – what they are saying about *your* business? All of these things are happening in the social space. Social gives you an opportunity to meet with them where they are.

Of course with every opportunity also comes some risk. More on that later, too.

What has social ever done for us?

We wanted to take the opportunity to share our personal stories, to illustrate what social media has done for us, our careers and our learning. The opportunities it has given to us, and can perhaps give to you too.

We are both experienced HR professionals. We first "met" on social media; Twitter to be precise. And then we met in real life, and this book, and a friendship, was born.

Gem's story

I sent my first tweet as @HR_Gem on 1 June 2011. Like many Twitter users I started off doing quite a bit of watching and looking. Or lurking, to give it its proper terminology. Just letting the content come to me and following HR people. When people join social networks there tends to be a bit of an evolution. Watching to begin with, followed by building up the confidence to go a little further; doing a little sharing and chatting. As people start to follow you back, you start to be more comfortable in beginning dialogue, and slowly move to a more active phase.

I started to chat regularly to people within the HR community. One day in February 2013, I tweeted about how nice it would be to meet some **tweeps** in the flesh, or as they say on Twitter, IRL (in real life). I found out about a networking event for people in HR and the like, organised via social media channels, called Connecting HR Manchester.

So I booked a hotel for the night and off I went. I suppose it was a bit like going on a blind date, only with 25 people. As the evening wore on, more and more rather awesome and interesting people turned up. It was HR, and it was social, and it was engaging. This is where I met Tim IRL for the first time, after tweeting each other since November 2012.

Of course, a drink was taken. Then we went to a chip shop, where four of us preceded to have a very heated debate about the future of employee voice post trade union decline. Then there was some arm wrestling. It was that sort of evening. But aside from the jokes, I made some excellent contacts that have turned into friendships, collaborations and all sorts of opportunities, including this very book.

Eventually I went on and started my blog, 'People Stuff'. I've gone on to blog from events, speak at conferences and at universities, and write for various magazines and websites. I've collaborated on eBooks, all though my social media connections. None of these opportunities would have happened but for social media. I have also been a state of almost continuous learning, beginning every morning when I check my timeline over the first coffee of the day. I have an amazing network and am part of a community, all in the device in my pocket.

Tim's story

I sent my first tweet as @TimScottHR on 1 November 2012. I was encouraged to tweet by a former colleague who told me he found it very useful professionally and thought I would too. For most of my career I'd operated as the "standalone" HR person in my organisation, which meant that apart from reading the odd magazine and attending the occasional employment law update, I didn't "network" with other HR people that much, so it seemed a good way to get involved with other people in my professional area and build up some contacts.

At this stage I have to confess that I'd actually had a different Twitter account since 2009. I did what seems to be mandatory for people joining Twitter in that I followed a few celebrities and a handful of people I knew. I didn't really "get" it to be honest and as a result I hardly ever checked it. It was only when I discovered the community of HR people that actively use it that it started to make sense. I think of it like learning a language – it takes a while to get your head around the general approach but once you've got a basic idea, the only way to develop is simply to dive in and get speaking it. You might make the odd grammatical mistake but native speakers will get what you mean and overlook the occasional mishap.

It isn't overstating it to say that since I joined Twitter, my career has been completely reinvigorated. Rather like Gem's story, sending that first tweet started a stone rolling that has seen me speaking at conferences, making videos for the CIPD, joining international project teams to improve the world of work, writing for HR publications and occasionally appearing in print media too! Oh and writing the odd book too. There are people I'm now proud to number amongst my closest friends who I would never have met without social media. I've also transformed how I approach my work – I'm convinced I got my current role largely on the strength of the knowledge and self-confidence (and the odd direct quote) I'd got from my social network. None of these things would have happened if I'd have carried on being that unintentionally insular HR person, closed away in my thinking and practice.

Although I'm yet to have a chip shop arm wrestle. There's still time...

P.S. We now live together. That isn't something you should necessarily expect to happen if you get into social leadership. But we aren't complaining.

The Social Leader

In this social world, the organisation is ever more transparent. Do you *need* to be on social media? Being completely honest, you probably don't (although if you stop reading at this point, you've probably wasted the cost of this book). But we believe it is an opportunity. The research shows that there are still plenty of leaders that aren't social. They think using social media means they have a LinkedIn account that they update once in a blue moon – probably when they are looking for a job opportunity. This ain't social leadership. The fact that so few leaders are genuinely social means that you can stand out in the crowd. Lead the way. Get ahead of the rest.

What do we mean by a 'social leader'? Simple. Someone who is actively using social media platforms to engage with their employees and customers alike. Someone who is genuinely and regularly present in the social world. Who knows that they are doing there and does it for themselves. Someone who shares their thoughts and ideas and is willing to enter into dialogue in this space. It is someone who is a leader for now and for the digital and social future.

The social leader still remains something of a rare thing. Research in 2014 into Fortune 500 companies found that two thirds of CEOs had no social presence at all. Those that did were mostly over on LinkedIn and not terribly active. A few had found their way over to Twitter but were tweeting about once a month. Not very social at all then really.

So what is stopping them? Firstly, there are a whole load of myths around social media, from the 'it will take too much time' excuse to the 'I don't know how to work it' cop out. Our later chapter on myth busting will hopefully put some of those to bed. But whatever the reason, it is a fact that, whilst there are some trailblazers doing good stuff, few business leaders are truly social ones. This presents an opportunity to get to the forefront – for those who are brave enough.

If you still need a little more convincing, here are just a few of the benefits we believe result from social leadership:

- Social media makes you a real person. The larger the organisation, the less likely it is that the average Executive or CEO can meet all of the people that work for them. Even in smaller companies it can be tough to find face time with people. But social media opens this up. You can be genuinely accessible to the people that work for you.

- Social media allows you to engage with and listen to your employees. Employee voice as a concept is changing. The employee engagement survey has had its day. Your people are now over on Glassdoor talking about what it is like to work for you. Engaging here will give you plenty of data about how people feel about working at your place.

- Social media allows consumers to build trust with a brand and to build long term relationships – no matter what size of organisation. This starts with the leader of that brand – you.

- Social media goes to where the consumers are, in the place that they are interacting every day. It allows you to engage with those groups and just maybe make them your fans or advocates.

- Social media makes your brand visible and enhances brand awareness – and by this we mean not only your corporate brand but your *personal brand* too.

- Social media is real time not slow time. Want to know what people are thinking? Ask. Now.

- Social allows you to position yourself and your business as an authority. Maybe even a thought leader.

- It helps with talent acquisition. Having a strong social leader tells a story in its own right about why people might want to come and work for you.

- It will help the organisation with social and digital skills. You have probably heard of the concept of 'the shadow of the leader'. Your employees need digital skills to survive in our new digital and social wold. By leading the way, you will encourage others to get social too.

- For the smaller company or the self-employed professional, social can get you a great web presence even if you haven't got a huge budget for marketing or a fancy website.

- Social media, especially blogging, is a great way of starting a conversation

- You can easily monitor your competitor activity, as well as listen to what people are saying about you and your brand in the social space.

Of course, if you don't get social then there are implications there too. Digital and social technologies can no longer be seen as just a trend or a fad. They are the way we live our lives. Those that fail to adapt will surely find themselves going the way of the dinosaur. The time of the social leader has come. It's time to hang back or get ahead.

Because a social leader needs a social organisation, we are devoting the next few chapters to looking at how you can get your place of work social too. Practical advice time coming up!

Social Media and the Organisation

Your organisation is probably already doing social media to some extent. Certainly your marketing team will be (we hope). There might well be a corporate Twitter account. A LinkedIn page. Instagram even. Depending on what sort of organisation you are, and how far along the social adoption curve you are, will depend on how social your organisation is.

But get beyond the brand stuff. Social selling and marketing does not make for a social organisation. What makes a social organisation is one in which social technology is not only used but understood, embraced, and embedded. Social leadership is the key to making this happen. It's that 'shadow of the leader' concept again: the idea that leaders cast a shadow across their organisations, intentionally or otherwise. Through your behaviour and language, through what you do and what you don't, as a leader you send strong signals about what is okay and what is not.

A social leader therefore sends a signal that it is ok for their employees to be social too. The right role model can make all the difference. When leaders embrace social, so will others.

Social media is fundamentally changing organisations and the way that we work.

First up is transparency. Information that used to be retained by just a few is now more available than ever. Take **Glassdoor**. If you haven't heard of it then it is worth a Google search. Because you don't know what is being said about your place. Glassdoor is a review site, on which employees and job seekers can talk about their experiences of working for you or the process of applying for a job with you. And the most interesting thing about it? Anyone can set up a page for your organisation. It doesn't need to be done by you or one of your marketing team. It might be a former employee, or even a job seeker that didn't get the role that they wanted.

People talk about everything on social media, including their work.

Take learning too. Social media has disrupted how people can learn. No longer do employees need to sit in a training course from 9-5. Instead they can access information that will help them do their job in real time.

We think this is so fundamental we've dedicated a whole chapter to it later.

Other social platforms such as **Slack** are designed for team working and collaboration. No longer do we need to send closed loop emails to everyone, cc-ing everyone "just for information", don't you know. We can work in real time using everything from instant messaging to **Wikis** to dedicated applications.

One of the biggest limitations to how much we make the most of the opportunities social technology presents us with, will be simply ourselves. It has been written that the future is a mirror in which we can only see ourselves. Find it hard to imagine a future without email? Probably because you use it all the time. Think you know how your customers like to buy from you? You are probably thinking about how they buy from you today, because that is the only way that they can. Think about HMV. Kodak. Even your local Woolworths. This is the mistake that they made. They only saw the future as it was right then. Don't make the same mistake in your leadership.

Social and digital technology is creating a different future, different ways of working and selling…. and has the power to change organisational culture. If we let it.

Social Media and Organisational Culture

Organisational culture: often talked about, less frequently understood.

It's sometimes described as 'the way we do things around here'.

What we do know about organisations is that culture is a big influence on what gets done, not to mention how and why.

We have worked in a fair few organisations between us. And in many of those organisations we have heard similar complaints.

Find us an employee survey where someone doesn't complain about communication in some way and we will eat our smartphones. Employees often talk about not knowing what is going on. About never seeing those in leadership roles. About silo working. About not being listened to.

Here's what we think: social media, when at its best and fully embedded can help influence and shift your culture.

It's about employee engagement.

It's about leadership.

It's about new ways of working.

It's about collaboration.

It is about, at heart, transparency.

First things first: communication. What is it like at your place? So much of what we call communication within organisations is basically a monologue. It is the company (and often not an individual) talking *at* the people who work for it. It is one way. Feedback mechanisms are usually weak. If there is a way of comment or responding, chances are it is a closed mechanism. For example, you have a question? Email it. And get an email response. Maybe. One to one.

Social is the very opposite. It is multi-directional. It is one to many. It is open and transparent. It provides the opportunity for that rarest of things within an organisation: dialogue.

Take this as an example.

The leader of an organisation blogs about his week. About the meetings they have attended. The customers or employees they have met. They put it out there on social. It can be read by those customers or employees alike. They can ask questions and directly get access to the writer. Everyone else can then see the ongoing conversation too. Join in or simply watch.

Or this one. Instead of running an employee engagement survey once a year, ask a different question every week on your internal social media network. Or run a poll. Let everyone see the comments and results in real time, rather than sending out a few summary PowerPoint slides when everyone has forgotten about it.

Or another. Next time you launch a project, don't do anything by email. Run the whole project through the most suitable app.

Or get on **Glassdoor** and respond to some comments about what it is like to work for you.

We could go on. And on.

Scary? Maybe. Different? For some.

This is the stuff that changes your culture. This is the stuff that will make you fit for the social and digital future that awaits us.

Is your organisation ready?

Getting the organisation involved

If one of your aims as a social leader is to engage with your people or change your culture, then this is the chapter for you.

We mentioned a little earlier that when it comes to technology, it is often said that there are two things that make a difference as to whether individuals adopt it or not: how easy it is to use, and the extent to which it is seen to solve a problem that the individual has (or to what extent it adds value for them). It's back to the old 'what's in it for me' routine.

We believe social media is easy to use…. after a little while. Yes, there is jargon. There are things that differ from platform to platform. There are the myths that many still believe. So, first things first. Training, training and more training.

You simply cannot overestimate its importance. If you want people to use social media you are going to have to help them learn the skills that will enable them to do so. This might take a little bit of time and effort. You can run some courses (we totally know people that do that. Ahem). Or you can simply find the champions that will already exist within your organisation. There will be people who are using social extensively in their personal or professional lives. So, get them on the case, acting as mentors or champions or guides. Call them what you like. Create a team. A stealth one if you must. And let them loose in your organisation with your blessing and encouragement. Of course, some of their managers might be laggards who want to tie them to a desktop, so don't forget you'll need some strategies to deal with that along the way.

You then need to address the 'what's is in it for me' for everyone else.

There are plenty of reasons to get social in this very book. For the organisation, there are a couple of approaches you can take. The first is big bang. If you haven't got one already, launch an internal social media network (see the next chapter for more on this!). If you have got one, assess how it is doing. Then own it. Use it. Get it moving and delivering using our handy advice guide that is coming up soon. Go out and tell people why you want to be a more social organisation. Share your social strategy. Do that training we mentioned earlier. Set objectives for the people that work for you. Share openly what, as a leader, your people

29

can expect from you and where they can find your stuff. Push social and push it hard.

The second is the slightly less in-your-face version. Just begin. Yourself. Engage those champions. Make sure your marketing, comms and HR teams are ready and aligned, if you have them. As they don't quite say in Frozen... let it grow.

You may also need to do a little myth busting (but don't worry, we have put most of typical ones into a handy chapter in this very book for your reading pleasure).

Our advice for getting the organisation involved is this:

- Meet people where they are in terms of their understanding and skill level.

- Don't assume that this will happen quickly. It won't.

- Role models will be needed. This starts with you.

- Take your time to make the case for social and why it is important for your wider organisation. Draw on the opportunities to sell, market and engage with customers. Pretty much everyone will get that aim even if they don't appreciate all the rest of it.

- Consider targeting sales and marketing people specifically. Frankly, we believe that any sales and marketing person who isn't all over social media in 2016 should be on a capability plan, but that may be just us. But you do need to question someone who isn't on LinkedIn. Just saying.

- Don't forget the training – and the supporting policy!

Some additional practical things you can do....

1. Run a competition via social media. Internal or external. Whatever works for you. Nothing too controversial. Best photo or video clip, ideas for naming the platform... anything that people might get engaged and talking.

2. Launch it properly. Decide in advance what your corporate social platform is all about – what you want from it. What sort of communication and information and conversation you are trying to encourage and where? This will help people get it and know what to go there for.

3. Drive people towards your internal social media platform – include links to it on emails and other methods of communication. Remind people of it at every opportunity (if you haven't got one, see the next chapter!)

4. Provide only certain types of information on your social platform. Nothing too important of course. But the fun stuff maybe, or the competitions.

5. Get those champions from within your organisation. A cross section of job types, departments and from across the traditional hierarchy is what you need. Get them sharing and encouraging others. Run a recruitment campaign internally. Make it fun, make it something people are excited to be involved in. Give them a team name, give them responsibility.

6. Be specific to other senior people in your organisation. Make sure they understand they need to be on there. Especially sales and marketing types. There should be no excuses.

7. Role model it (this means you, social leader). Did we already say that?

8. Keep up with the other methods of communications too. Social won't work for everybody. You won't convert every employee. So just as with the marketing stuff, keep up a mix.

One of the most useful things that you can do to take your organisation social, is launch an enterprise social network, or ESN. And luckily for you, this is coming up in the next chapter.

Finally.... Keep on going. It will take time.

Enterprise Social Networks

Enterprise Social Network, or ESN, is a fancy name for what is basically a social media platform where membership is limited to your own organisation and employees. Yammer is one of the most popular examples. Facebook at Work (now called Workplace by Facebook), only recently launched at the time we are writing this book, is likely to be highly influential in this space in the very near future.

First things first. You need an internal email address. And yes, we do still meet companies where not everyone has one. Just let that sink in for a minute...

You don't need much else to begin. Just make sure it isn't blocked on the corporate network. Make sure that the social media policy is up to date and good to go, and find someone who can take overall ownership of the platform internally (in so far as anyone can ever 'own' social).

Hopefully you have already read the earlier chapter on getting your organisation involved in social media. There is (at least) one thing that we do know for certain about ESNs and that is this: build it and they will not come. Most internal social networks do not, in our experience, live up to their potential. You can have the best site in the world. You can pay for enhanced functionality. You can put in a whole load of effort. But it won't take off by itself.

There are a few reasons for this. The good news is that with some time and effort all the issues that prevent adoption can be overcome. We've already mentioned the stuff about adoption of technology and what makes people engage... or otherwise.

People will fall into several categories when you try and launch an internal social network.

First up will be the folk who dislike everything that the organisation does, whether it is social media or frankly anything else. Just ignore those people. They are not your target market.

Second, will be the people who don't get social media or why they might want to be on it, or believe all of the myths (see the myths chapter coming up soon).

Then there will be the people who 'don't have time'. We've already talked about this on our myth busting chapter. These people will say too, that they don't have time to read the company magazine, or indeed engage with any communication you do as a leader and will then complain they don't know anything.

There are those that will join an internal network but will only lurk – read other people's stuff but don't comment. Don't worry about this too much. Some people just aren't comfortable with joining in but if they are consuming content, that is just fine.

Then there will be the people managers. Those that aren't fans of social themselves or think that social media means, well, social stuff, may well try and stop their people using it. Or tell them they can only use it outside of working hours. You may need to be very explicit to your leadership community that this is now an accepted part of the day job. That communicating and sharing and learning is part of their job too.

There are the folk that join the network and then are never seen again. Then there are the grumps that just refuse to join it at all.

Oh, and there will be people that love it and get it and share and learn and collaborate. We love these people.

This isn't meant to sound overly negative. But you will come across these people if you try launch and embed social. Our advice is this...

- Focus on those people initially that are getting it and joining in. leverage them at every opportunity.

- Follow our earlier advice for getting the organisation involved.

- Tackle the groups and individuals described above one at a time. Training will address some of it. Role modelling will address others.

- Address the people manager stuff early on. Consider doing this formally, in person. Make sure that they know telling people they can only go on the network during their lunch break is no longer acceptable.

- Remember the app. It isn't just about the desktop version. Making the content accessible when people want to see it. You can't expect or force people to read and engage with work content when they are at home. But make it a place of interesting conversation and content (see next point!) then they might just do it anyway.

- Share good content – this is the key to engagement!

- Don't sweat the small stuff. You won't convert everyone, just like you can't get everyone to read the company newsletter (if you still do such a thing).

There are examples out there of companies that have used internal social networks to great effect. A Google search will take you to some of them.

PS. If you need any help with launching your internal social media network, or training your people let us know. That is what we do. #shamelessplug #sorrynotsorry

Social Selling

Here's another reason why leaders need to be social: every organisation needs to sell *something* (even if it's just their own competence) and manage a brand.

Social media has changed the sales and marketing landscape and disrupted the traditional sales cycle. We still believe we have only seen a small part of the potential. More is still to come.

People buy online, of course. But even if they don't always complete the transaction there, our purchasing decisions are hugely influenced in the online space all the same. We check out **crowdsourced** product reviews (think Trip Advisor); we listen to what our friends say online.

In the old days, marketing had the consumer in very much a passive, receiving sort of space. Whether it was a TV advert broadcasting at you while you sat on the sofa, a mass-mailed press release, a billboard at the side of the road or junk mail through the letter box, they sent and you received. The brand told you that they were awesome. You might buy or you might not. If you bought and you liked it, you might buy some more and you might tell a few of your friends.

Consumer behaviour has changed. We are much more active than we used to be, in terms of our purchasing behaviour, our interactivity with brands and our public willingness to share our consumer experiences – the good and the bad. Social media means that there is interaction taking place, between the buyer and the seller. It has also increased the power of that consumer, who can take that action anywhere and any when. Now, you want other people to tell other people you are awesome. Let's face it, who are you more likely to believe – the corporate message, or your friend that just used the product?

Social media is influencing our buying decisions like never before. It is also changing our consumer behaviour in other ways. We learn about products, brands and services through our social feeds. We complain about poor service, including the offending company in the tweet. We are exposed to celebrities waxing lyrical about their favourite brands. We have more information at our finger tips than we ever have had.

So, like with all things social, there is an opportunity and there is a risk.

The opportunity is to engage with your customers and potential customers in a totally new way. More interactive, more dialogue, more about building a long-term relationship. A way to build your brand, showcase your products and services, tell your stories. Social media can give your brand a personality; make it come to life beyond the corporate, often formal messaging. Social becomes the face of your brand and your story, just like the shop assistant in the high-street store or the receptionist at corporate HQ. Of course, as a leader, this brand face, this image and story can come to life through you too, and not just the corporate social feeds.

The risks are many too. Employees can damage your brand – and so could you if you get it wrong. Take the example of a clothing brand American Apparel. Their (young) social media manager tweeted a picture of the exploding space shuttle Challenger on the 4th July. He'd just been looking for an image. An image that was immediately recognisable as something terrible, to people of a certain age. Lesson: don't hand your social media account over to inexperienced people just because they are young and therefore must understand it. And as you will see when we come onto our rules for social media for leaders in the very next chapter, we recommend not handing over your personal social media to anyone else at all.

Here's another example of how social media and give you a good kick in the corporate rear when you least expect it. In 2008, a United Airlines passenger saw baggage handlers throwing his guitar onto a plane. When he retrieved it, the guitar was damaged. He asked the airline to pay for the damage caused, but they refused. So the passenger wrote a song about it, and posted the video on You Tube. To date, it has had over 14 million views. That same passenger then wrote a book about the experience and is now a conference speaker. The lesson here is that social media can seriously damage you too; if you give crappy customer service, you might just go viral.

What we are saying is this: whilst you will struggle to find two people who love social as much as we do, we recognise that it isn't a panacea. It isn't the answer to everything. And you need to understand and manage the risks if you get involved.

Here are some of those risks:

- Doing social badly, whether as a leader or an organisation, is worse than not doing it at all. This includes not being sufficiently present, either in terms of content provision, but also in terms of responding to questions or comments.

- You need to be fast to respond to your customers and your employees especially to anything negative. Otherwise it looks like you are hiding and has a negative impact on your perceived authenticity.

- It needs to be maintained – from a business perspective, content, as they say, is king. You continually need to put good, relevant content out there for people to see. Once a month won't cut it.

- Poor content can damage your brand – personal or corporate.

- If you offer poor customer service, poor value for money and the like, this will surface on social. But it will do that whether you are there or not.

There is one important point that can be a risk if you get it wrong at the outset. When it comes to marketing, social media is one part of the marketing mix and the overall strategy. It is an "as well as" and not instead of. If you treat it as an entirely separate thing, you will never fully exploit its potential.

At the risk of repeating ourselves: in social media, there is both new opportunity and new risk. One of the people we admire in this space is Gary Vaynerchuck, and he has a great message that we think is relevant here. He says that you need to market your business in the year that you are living in. And frankly, that means socially.

One final point. It is 2016. There is no excuse for your sales teams not to be all over social media. Are they? If you don't know, maybe it is time to go and find out. And if they are not, if you forgive us for another mention of it, it is training time...

Social Media for Learning

Just because you've bagged a seat at the boardroom table, it doesn't mean that you are done learning and developing. Although the busier you get the harder it can be to find the time.

But a solution is at hand. And yes, it is social media.

Training used to mean going on a course. Sitting listening to an expert at the front of the room. They usually had PowerPoint. A workbook perhaps. There would almost certainly be biscuits. It was a 9-5 kind of thing (and yes, we know you were hoping for an early finish – let's just work through the afternoon tea break).

Not anymore.

How and when you learn can be fundamentally changed by social media. For you, and for the people that work for you.

Take your phone. We are guessing that like more than half of the population you might well have a smart phone. Maybe you still even use it for actual phone calls (do tell us what that is like). But phones are no longer just phones. They are for shopping and for directions. They are for banking and for talking to our friends and for finding the nearest coffee shop. For job hunting or for monitoring how far we walked today or taking photos. You get our drift.

Pretty much everything you could ever want to know is on the device in your pocket.

Just think about that for the moment.

Through a Google search, you could probably learn anything or everything.

And you could be sat on the toilet while you are learning it, and no one will even know (note from Gem – this is officially known as "Poogling". Don't ask me how I know this).

If you want a little bit of leadership wisdom, watch a Ted Talk.

If you want to know the meaning of something, try Wikipedia.

Want to improve your fitness levels? Read a running blog.

Want to find other people talking about what you do? Join a Twitter chat or a LinkedIn group.

It is all there. People putting stuff out online. Sharing their thoughts, their work, their presentations. Their ideas. And yes, probably occasionally their breakfast too. But a little bit of personal on social never hurt: it helps to make you a real person.

So, if you want to learn stuff, keep up to date in your field, then social media is one way to do just that. Accessible whenever you need it.

Think too about what this means for the people who work for you. Your organisation might not have a big training budget. You might not have people working in Human Resources who are dedicated to helping others learn or delivering training. But get your organisation social, provide the right skills and signpost the way and all the learning you need is right there in the social world. Even better, this is much better aligned to how people actually learn in real life. There is plenty of research out there that confirms we don't retain all that much when we go on one of those formal 9-5 training courses. If we don't immediately put that new knowledge into use when we get back to the day job, then we remember even less.

You do this in your private life, don't you? Ever followed a Nigella recipe on YouTube? Looked up something on Wikipedia? You don't book yourself a training course for that stuff.

This is learning *in the moment*. Learning when we need to access the knowledge and are about to use it. Reading, watching, engaging with the content. Sharing it with others and engaging in dialogue. This is when and how we learn and when we retain knowledge.

If you have a Human Resources team, or someone responsible for learning at your place, then you had better make sure they get social. Because the learning of today and tomorrow can and will be different. Less content creation and more curation of stuff that is already out there: useful, interesting and easy to consume. So, one more thing you might want to do after reading this little book is check out the social media skills of your people people. If they don't have them, then it is time for a conversation.

In an earlier chapter, we talked about Enterprise Social Media platforms - internal social media just for your organisation. This is most definitely a place where learning can take place in just the way we have described, with the right kind of support and guidance. Just one of the many ways you can release the potential for internal social media is to make it a hub for learning and interesting stuff.

So, what you are waiting for?

Myth Busting

Now before we get too much further into this book, there are some elephants in the room that we need to deal with. We find that when we meet people who know that we are self-confessed social media addicts, we get asked lots of the same questions and are on the receiving end of lots of the same comments. We also get lots of reasons why people say that they can't do social. Typically, we give pretty much the same responses – to conference delegates, followers on Twitter and leaders alike. So here are our responses to the same old same old......

I don't have the time.

The answer to this one is simple. If you want to do something enough, then you will find a way and make the time. And, as the saying goes, if you don't, you will find an excuse. That is why there are usually more people down the pub than in the gym. If you take the time to master the skills, then it won't take too much time at all.

I know I should give it a go.

Usually said in the same tone of voice we use when we ponder tackling our household chores. See our earlier comment on doing stuff that you want to do. Here's the thing – if you are thinking about getting social, you must know why you are doing it. Because if you don't have a good why, an aim, then you will find it hard to be motivated to get going or keep going. Our why is simple. We use social media to learn from others, to make great connections, to chat to friends and to get updates on One Direction (note from Tim – just to remind you, that last one is just Gemma). If you want to be a social leader, then be one. Simple.

Isn't Twitter just about people saying what they had for breakfast?

No.

I don't know what to say.

Don't worry about it too much. You manage to have conversations with people at work all day, right? You are not crafting a novel. Just stay away from the obvious inflammatory stuff. If you worry about it, overthink it, you will never do it.

Social media is a confidentiality risk to my business.

Most of your employees are not stupid. They aren't likely to start tweeting your trade secrets or posting your payroll data on Facebook.

Employees will do stupid stuff on social media.

Despite what we said above, some employees will do stupid things. They always have done. Social media is just where it might show up these days. It isn't the cause. If it happens, deal with it. Better still, do what you can to avoid it in the first place by providing guidelines and training.

How do you cope with the constant stream of stuff coming at you?

Cognitive overload is a real thing. And it's not just about social media. Emails, phone calls, text messages, voicemails, instant messages, alerts, notifications. We are constantly connected, constantly interrupted. You can find a way to manage the social stuff just like you do with the rest of it. In Twitter, you can use lists. Some people use apps or feeds for collation or to make sure they don't miss something important to them. You also should be selective on who you follow and what you read, or you could easily be overwhelmed. You can't catch every tweet so don't even try – it simply isn't meant to be used that way.

I don't know how to do it. There is all this terminology that I don't understand.

It takes a little getting used to, just like anything new. But it isn't all that hard, if you want to learn it. When it comes to HR there is a welcoming community who will help you along the way. Plus, you now have a handy glossary at the back of this book to help.

Isn't it a bit sad?

This all depends on your point of view. Nothing is sad if you get some benefit from it or enjoy it. Can you take it too far? Yes of course you can. There is balance in all things, including social media. But to us there is nothing sad about learning, reading, collaborating or chatting to our friends.

Isn't it just for the younger generation?

Nope. It is true that the younger you are, the more you have grown up with this stuff, the more it is second nature. For those currently at school, there was no time before the internet or the mobile phone. But writing it off as something for those pesky kids is both dangerous and inaccurate. The evidence points to the fact that it simply isn't the case and in the case of some social media platforms, the fastest growing demographic is the older generation. It looks like you can teach an old dog new tweets.

Employees will misuse it / spend too much time on it.

They might. See the earlier point. And to the point about time..... time spent communicating and sharing with colleagues isn't a waste of time. To those who might be messing about on Facebook – well employees have always found ways to waste time. Extra-long smoke breaks, extending the lunch hour by five minutes here and there. If this is taking place, you have other problems rather than social media.

It doesn't apply to us / me / our business.

Whether we like it or not, believe it or not, social is the new normal. This is the world that we live in, today and tomorrow. It isn't going anywhere. The individual platforms might come and go, trends will rise and fall, but we live in a mobile, connected, digital world. Your customers are there, your employees are there, and your friends are there. You can choose if you want to be there too. And it is a choice. But there are risks with not engaging too.

Adoption of Social

You may be already familiar with Roger's Innovation Adoption Curve (revisit the chapter on learning and Google it if not!).

It measures the extent to which innovations flow through society. Most things, especially technology, tend to follow a similar pattern both in society and within organisations. Early on is the innovator and the early adopter; those folks who are ahead of the curve and want the new stuff first. They are the ones queuing up all night outside a store getting the latest gadget so they have their hands on it as soon as the doors open. Everyone else slowly catches up at a varying pace, eventually landing with the late majority and then the laggards who catch up last of all.

So, if you are a leader and you want to encourage your employees to get involved, it might take a little time and some express permission from you and your teams.

How to spot a laggard:

- They see no reason to upgrade their Nokia 3210

- When you ask them if they saw your instant message, they ask you what one of those is

- They have used a fax machine (probably in the last week)

- They make comments like 'isn't Twitter all about telling people what you had for breakfast'.

We jest. A little. We are probably in the middle of this journey when it comes to social media. It has been around for some time. For many people and organisations, it has been part of their everyday life for some time. For others, it is still a world of strange language and something for "the kids".

There are a couple of things that usually impact upon how well technology is adopted both within an organisation and personally too. There is something called the Technology Adoption Model. Not everyone likes it, and it has been criticised as being too simplistic. But we think it works for the social world. The first thing that impacts adoption, or otherwise, of social media, is the extent to which people see the benefit to themselves – what problem is it solving? The official model calls it 'perceived usefulness'. We tend to think of it as the 'What's in it for me' (WIIFM) question.

And the WIIFM will vary from person to person.

What all of this means, is that your customers and employees will be adopting social media in a similar way. Some will be using it excessively and have fully incorporated it into their lives. Like us, they will spend quite a bit of time looking on their phones. For others, they aren't there all that much at all. This is why you still need to maintain a mix of all marketing approaches. For as much as we are advocates of all things social, it cannot ever be the full solution.

P.S. When considering the adoption of social, it might just be worth checking that the company laggard isn't you... You don't still have a Nokia 3210 – do you??

Employee Advocacy

We think this is so important we are going to dedicate a whole little chapter to it.

Simply put, employee advocacy is the promotion of an organisation by its own employees: the people who work for you sharing your content across their own networks *because they want to*. From an employer brand perspective, this is perhaps the ultimate goal. Research shows that people trust real life reviews and the opinions of "average employees" over corporate and senior executive messages every time, in much the same way that people are influenced by reviews on sites likes Amazon or TripAdvisor.

If you're lucky, your employees may already be sharing your content. This is a massive opportunity for your organisation. Think brand. Think recruitment. Think reputation. Think how much more real - and potentially cost effective – this is than the other stuff in your marketing mix.

Having a strategy and formalised approach could help to maximise your efforts.

Consider this ideal scenario: your employees, sharing your messaging with their friends and family, on the social media network of their choice – without prompting (or bribing!), talking positively about what it is like to work for you or your products and services. Employee advocacy is essentially harnessing the power of word of mouth – social media style.

Of course, the whole point of employee advocacy is that it needs to be organic. You can't really force it, and if you try it may well backfire on you. But it is something that you can encourage and make easier for people. So, if you want to engage your employees and their social networks, here are five considerations specifically about employee advocacy:

1. **Make it easy** for employees to share your stuff. Send them updates; make it clear not only that they can share this information but that you would positively welcome it. Include sharing buttons for relevant sites – this is practical but important.

2. Don't just tell your people that you are happy for them to share – **provide guidance** too! Some employees will need to expressly be told that you want them to share company messages. Of course, you want content to be shared in an effective way that appropriately represents your brand. We've talked elsewhere in this little book about social media policies so we won't repeat ourselves – but don't forget that thing about permission.

3. **Reward advocacy**. This doesn't necessarily mean providing excessive or monetary rewards – this might of course generate the wrong behaviours. But a thank you, especially a social media one, goes a long way and reinforces the desired behaviours.

4. Get some **role models**. This isn't specific to employee advocacy. This is essentially what the whole book is about. But you and your other leaders will need to send a message that sharing on social networks is not only acceptable but actively encouraged if you really want people to get social. But as well as leaders, consider engaging some champions across the organisation. Find out who is already very social, connected or influential and get them involved and part of the team.

5. **Train your people on social media**. You already know this isn't just specific to advocacy, obviously but if you really want to get people social you will need to spend some time explaining what is in it for them to get social and provide practical help on how to do so. You'll also be helping them to find a potential source of professional knowledge – but you've already read that chapter.

Employee advocacy has the potential be a huge boost to your branding efforts. But ultimately it will only happen if your organisation is a good place to work. If your employees aren't willing to share your content or express their pride in working for you, then you might have a bigger cultural problem to consider...

Where you have advocates you can also have detractors. People will happily talk about the negative side of your organisation too, whether that is about what it is like to work for you, your customer service, your products and so on. You can't control this. But you can respond to negative online reviews and comments in a constructive manner. An apology never hurt anyone.

Them's the rules.

We hope that you are starting to understand our philosophy about social media and why we believe it is so important. Coming up now are a few chapters on practical stuff: advice, tips, guidance. First up, some of our recommended rules for social, to the extent that there are any.......

Rule Number One: Be sensible

You can think what you like. You can say what you like. You can pretty much say what you like on social media too, unless you are breaking the law. But a little common sense would tell you that publicly broadcasting whatever comes to mind, especially when it includes expletives, obscenities and insults, pictures of you under the influence or anything containing discrimination, nudity or the like is going to cause you an issue if that particular account is linked in any way to your job. What can make your personal brand can break it too. This sounds obvious but plenty of people get it wrong all the same. History is replete with people who have posted a social media status in haste and repented at leisure.

Common sense. Something that should be exercised alongside your social media use at all times. People have varying standards on social media, as they do in all aspects of life. We quite like the approach of one of our mutual tweeps which is to ask himself before tweeting:

- Would it offend my Mum?

- What would my boss think?

Oh - and never, ever tweet whilst drunk. It won't end well.

Rule Number Two: Pick your platforms

You can't do it all. You will need to pick your platforms. Better to do a couple really, really well, and build up a following, than try to do ten platforms averagely. Our thoughts on that are coming up soon.

Rule Number Three: Take people with you

If your organisation isn't very social right now you might need to spend some time explaining why you are doing this. Even providing some basic training and a policy (you can contact me if you need any help with this!).

Training is key. Once people understand the why, help them with the how. Social can feel scary when you first use it. Although to some people it is part of their everyday, there are others to whom it is completely new. People worry about what to tweet, what they can and can't share. Social is full of new terminology and involves technology that is unfamiliar to some. So, make it easy for folks to get on board and join in. The glossary at the back of this book will help!

You are the leader, so be the role model — especially if you are the business leader. Leaders getting in there and getting sharing can send the message that this is an okay way to spend your time at work.

Rule Number Four – Do it Yourself

This is your voice. Don't outsource it to someone else in the office: it will be obvious. This is about you being real and authentic.

Rule Number Five - Think carefully about personal versus private

If you are using social media for your business, then you might want to think about separating it entirely from any personal accounts. We've seen people who use their business Facebook account as their personal one too. But do you really want people who look you up as they are interested in working for or with you, finding some pictures of you out with your mates, or perhaps photos of your children. It doesn't look professional, and it doesn't set the right tone.

When you are deliberately keeping accounts private as they are nothing to do with your business or brand, then consider carefully your privacy settings. If someone goes a Google search of your name or company name, you want them to find your professional activities and shares, and not some drunken photos on your personal Facebook page.

Rule Number Six - What goes on social media, stays on social media.

You can delete stuff, but this doesn't make it disappear, as many celebrities will know to their cost. Anyone can take a screen shot of what you have tweeted or shared. Take care, don't get into arguments with trolls and stupid people, don't share things without reading them first, and stay away from anything like risky jokes, bad language or something that might be offensive.

Rule Number Seven - Listen

Social is a two-way dialogue. That means it isn't just about broadcasting your point of view but listening too. This is about your opportunity to listen to, and engage with, your employees and customers in a whole new way.

Rule Number Eight – Make it a habit

The more you do something, the more it becomes part of your established routine. A social leader can't just tweet a couple of times a month. This is about making real time for real engagement.

Rule Number Nine – Be authentic

As we have already said, this is your voice. It is about being you. This is what will make success of your social efforts. Anyone can smell corporate bullshit.

Getting Started

We have talked about the what and the why of social media. If you have read this far then we hope that we have convinced you of the need to be a social leader. Hopefully too you're feeling encouraged to have a go if you don't already, so now it is time to talk about the how - what you need to think about when getting social yourself or where you work. We are going to start with some of our top tips, and then dig a little deeper into a few.

First things first

Whether you are looking at social in an individual, leadership or a business context, any social media strategy should start with one question: *why*?

There are plenty of people having a go at social media, business leaders or otherwise. Some of them are doing it because they think they should or because everyone else is doing it. But without a clearly defined 'why' then it will be difficult to get the most from it and focus your efforts. Neither will it be easy to measure results and adapt your approach accordingly.

If it is on the personal side, maybe it is about improving (or establishing) your personal brand, or maybe you are initially just looking to get social for fun. For a leader, it could be about supporting the company brand or sales and marketing efforts, or engaging with customers or employees in a different way. Whatever it is, you need to come up with some aims and desired outcomes. Everything else flows from there. Without a why, it's a bit like just jumping on a bandwagon, and your efforts won't be sufficiently focused or your outcomes capable of review.

Firstly, decide why you are doing it at all. This doesn't need to be huge. Some small goals at first are just fine. Maybe begin with this question: *what sort of social leader do you want to be?*

Our other warning, especially if you are thinking about what social means for you and our business, is that you will need to make an investment in social, whether in time, resources or money. There is nothing worse in the land of social media than looking up a company or individual and finding an abandoned profile, or sending a tweet to them and hearing nothing back.

Just because most social media is free to sign up, there is sometimes the misconception that it is cheap and it is easy. Well this ain't necessarily so. Doing social well takes time and effort and return on investment isn't all that straightforward either.

Set your goals, and keep them under review. Then then set some more when you have reached them.

Oh. And make sure you have read our rules chapter before you send your first tweet!

Picking Your Platforms

As we said earlier, there are many, many forms of social media, and it is a developing space.

We can't cover them all in this book, and neither can you.

Our advice is always the same. Pick a couple of platforms that suit your business, and do them really well. Over the next few pages, we are going to take a few of the options and go into a bit more detail on them, as well as offering some tips and things to think about when deciding which ones to do. We'll look at the big platforms that you should be considering, and give you some ideas on how to do each. Note, this is the biggest chapter: you might want to get a cup of tea before beginning this one.

Twitter

We are both big advocates of Twitter. If we were to suggest that there is a platform that you definitely should be on, it is this one. A quick recap – Twitter is about sharing stuff in no more than 140 characters. You can include images or links in your tweets. The aim is to share stuff that is short and sharp. There are businesses of all shapes and sizes on Twitter. In fact, it is unusual to find a business that is not on Twitter today. We're such big fans, we've included a "How to get started on Twitter" section right at the back of this book in case you don't already have an account.

Top Tips for Twitter:

- Tweets do not have a long life, as people just don't scroll too far back. It's totally acceptable to share links to your content several times. So tweet regularly. You will need to be tweeting often – at least several times a day.

- If you can't be on the platform often enough, you can use an app (for example, TweetDeck or Hootsuite) to schedule tweets to go out at set times. Use this approach carefully though. Some people and organisations have run into difficulties with tweets that were scheduled long in advance but a major world event happened and they were suddenly inappropriately timed. Something to be aware of!

- Mix it up. Tweet links and images. Don't just tweet your own stuff, share from others too. (We will be saying this a lot).

- Engage. Through using the @ function, you can engage with others

- Use hashtags. You can make up your own, or check out what relevant ones already exist that are relevant to you. You don't have to do anything to set up a hashtag, you simply type it. You can even create one just for your business if you want.

- Re-tweet (also known as "RT"ing) other people as a way of engaging with them.

LinkedIn

The professional networking site. Like many sites, it has a 'freemium' model, which means that there is stuff that you can get for free, and other stuff that you can pay for. For example, on LinkedIn, you can pay for an enhanced profile or paid for job advertising.

There are two board options on LinkedIn. One is to have a personal profile, the other is to have a company profile. For the small business or self-employed practitioner, we recommend just having a good personal profile.

Company pages are great, but the free ones are very limited in terms of what you can do on them apart from sharing updates. There is an option to have a paid for company page

Top Tips for LinkedIn

- Have a complete profile – including a professional headshot. This is not the place for wedding photos, car pictures or cropped photos from a night out. A proper photograph is an investment, so have one taken if you don't already have one. As for the wider profile, LinkedIn will prompt and guide you on what areas need to be completed.

- Get recommendations for your work. Recommendations are a visible testimonial and reasons why people should choose to work with you and your business. Don't be afraid to ask people to write one. The worst thing that they can do is ignore you!

- Keep it professional! There are people who confuse LinkedIn with other, less formal sites. It's not the place to post personal stuff - people might choose to disengage with you. Save it for Facebook!

- Don't spam people! This is another big problem with the platform in our opinion. You connect with someone and then they start adding you to their mailing list or sending you links to their products straight away.

- Do join (relevant) groups, and take part in discussions. This is a good way to build new connections and increase visibility of your profile.

- As with all the platforms, as well as sharing your own stuff, share other people's too.

Facebook

The most commonly used platform still. Over one and a half billion members worldwide. So not a bad place to be thinking about building your personal or company profile. Facebook is more informal than other networks. It isn't really the sort of place that you go looking for products, businesses and suppliers. For the most part, people go there to chat to friends, keep in touch, share pictures and the like. Users are more likely to stumble upon something or someone, unless we are talking about promoted posts. You will often find, in the middle of your feed or along the side on a desktop, products and services that you might be interested in. Often, they are just the things that you have been looking at over on your Amazon or eBay accounts. They will be paid-for adverts, following you around the web based on your previous searches. You can have these but they can be super expensive.

Top Tips for Facebook:

- As we have included in one of our rules – never mix up your personal and professional Facebook profiles! Your clients and employees probably do not want to see your baby photos.

- Facebook has algorithms that chose what people see in their feed so you can't guarantee that your post will be seen by your followers, so regularity is important here too.

- Engage with your followers. This might just be responding to comments, but also consider posting a question or a poll to get people talking to you. Depending on how their privacy settings are organised, this should mean that you are seen in the feeds of the friends of your followers.

- You can use Facebook's own tools to analyse when your followers are active on the platform, so you can target your posts accordingly.

- Mix it up to grow your followers. Don't just do text posts, include videos, pictures and links.

Instagram

Instagram is an image sharing site for photos and video. Images are great as they often get more interaction than plain old text posts. Images can tell a story about your organisation, as well as showcase your products and services.

With one additional click you can also share them straight onto other platforms. Instagram is great for any business, but will be particularly good for anyone with a very visual product, so think cakes, clothing, home decoration and the like. You can also share pictures of your people or your premises.

Top Tips for Instagram:

- Post at least once a day.

- Use the filters that are available in the app to improve the pictures – just play around, it is quite user friendly.

- Engage with people that comment on your photos – reply and follow them back.

- Link Instagram up to your other accounts like Facebook or Twitter to share on multiple platforms all at once.

- Use humour and fun (and hashtags) in your images: they will get good engagement and give your brand a personality.

- Have a good profile and bio (applies to most of these sites!).

Pinterest

The easiest way to think about Pinterest is like a big online notice board. It is image-based, with the ability to share links and videos too. Users create 'boards' on which they 'pin' images that they like or want to share.

There is a Pinterest board for pretty much everything. From wedding dresses to health and fitness. From recipes to tattoo designs. From your favourite band to leadership quotes.

Pinterest is fab for showcasing what you do, especially if it is a visual product. For example, if you run a wedding business, you could have a board showing wedding dresses, another for flowers and another for bridesmaid outfits. If you are a photographer, you could show samples of your work. If you are a small business, you could show pictures of your premises and your team.

The benefit of Pinterest is that it is very easy to take a photograph on your phone, and upload it to the platform. You can put a link to the boards on your website, or simply occasionally tweet links to it…. 'Check out our Pinterest Boards here for more images of our products'.

You don't necessarily need to worry about building a following, because you can just direct people to the site for a good look around at any point in time.

Top Tips for Pinterest:

- Organise your content into easily understood 'boards'

- Unless you are pinning a heck of a lot, you might find it hard to get followers just based on your feed. You might be best thinking of Pinterest as a showcase to which you can direct people

- Follow other people – they might just follow you back!

- Keep your eye on interactions – you will find a 'you' section as well as a 'messages' section. The 'you' will show you anyone who has saved or liked your pins. The messages are, as indicated, messages directly to you from other pinners

- This is a site where you want to concentrate on sharing your own stuff, rather than other people's. Firstly, you don't always know the source or copyright of images on somewhere like Pinterest, and you don't want to get yourself in legal hot water. But as per the point above – because this is a primarily image site, this is a place to showcase your work, not someone else's

- Make sure you put descriptions on your pins to say exactly what they are. Also add a web link that will take people straight to your website

- Get creative with your images! There are fun and cheap apps that you can use to put text over your pictures. Try Wordswag as a simple to use option.

YouTube

You might not always think of YouTube as social media. It is the second biggest search engine in the world and also features heavily in Google search results. It is also a social platform in that it allows people to share from it and comment on posts. Getting videos on YouTube could be a real opportunity depending on the type of business you run. You can set up your own You Tube channel for free and include your own branding. It is great for visual content, and the beauty is that whatever you share on YouTube can also be shared across your other platforms.

Options could include; putting clips of you talking about your role or organisation, videos of your premises, or your products in manufacture.

Top Tips for YouTube:

- Keep it short to ensure that viewers don't disengage part way through your video.

- Name and describe your videos well, so that they will show up in organic search results, not just people who get referred from your other feeds.

- You can pay to have professional videos shot and edited. But this might prove too expensive. You can do your own, if you own a reasonable video camera. Don't forget most smartphones these days will shoot video in HD and the video is only likely to be viewed on the same sized screen – it doesn't have to IMAX 3D! It is okay to talk straight to camera for something like a vlog

- There is so much content uploaded to YouTube every day that you might not get high views with addition promotion. Share your video links everywhere!

- Make sure you use your brand logo on the site (same goes for all platforms really)

- Don't add music unless you have permission – or it is copyright free

- If you go onto YouTube itself, there are step by step tutorials on how to upload content and create your own channel

Snapchat

The idea behind Snapchat is to share images that are short-lived – both pictures and videos. Once seen, they disappear. Videos last up to 10 seconds in length, and then disappear after a single viewing. Said to have 150 million active daily users. Still overall something of a niche platform with a much younger demographic – but growing quickly. Definitely a platform to watch for the future. In 2016 it hit 10 billion daily video views.

How to decide….

When it comes to deciding which of these platforms to focus on, the most important questions to ask yourself are: *Where are your customers? Where are your employees? Where are the people you want to engage with? What are the social media networks that they are using?* You may be able to research these things, by asking existing customers or employees. Some Google searching might also give you some pointers. Or you simply might need to experiment for a while to see what gives you the best results and adapt accordingly.

We do know this – you probably can't do all of them really well. Instead pick a couple, and put effort into those and making them rock.

A few facts that might help you decide:

- Instagram and Pinterest work best for brands, people and businesses with very visual content. Pizza is the most Instagrammed food! Think about to what extent you want people to see you as a person before taking a decision on a visual approach

- Facebook is still the biggest platform in the world – and it continues to grow. If Facebook's users constituted a country, it would now be the largest one in the world. The average user has over 300 friends, meaning it is highly likely that at least some of the people you want to engage with are here, whether that is about you engaging as a leader in your own right or for your businesses marketing efforts

- Twitter users typically expect a response from a brand that they tweet within one hour. We think pretty much every organisation should have a Twitter account. You are missing out otherwise, as many consumers will expect you to have one. Twitter's wide appeal means it is also a good place for you to have a personal account too, if this is the choice you are making

- 90% of Instagram users are under 30. Pinterest has a more female user base. It is always worth asking yourself who the target consumers of your content are... and then checking out the demographic usage of the platforms you are considering using

- Snapchat is the third most popular app amongst 18-34 year olds (still behind Facebook and Instagram)

Whichever you go with, be prepared to change. Networks rise and fall in popularity, and demographics change too, not to mention new platforms arising regularly. So keep up with the trends!

And finally…. whichever platform you choose, make sure that you are sharing and updating regularly. In the world of social media, there is nothing worse than an abandoned social profile – with the sole exception of not having one at all!

More practical stuff

You've read the rules. You've picked your platforms. The accounts are good to go. And in no particular order, here's some other stuff we recommend doing, and some stuff we don't:

- Get some dialogue going. Maybe it's a poll on Twitter. It could be posing a question for comments, or contributing to one that is already happening in a relevant group. Respond to the people who talk to you in the social space.

- Share your own knowledge and ideas. Chances are, whatever it is you do, you know something that others don't, or would find interesting. Check out our dedicated chapter on blogging for more on how you can do this.

- Share often. Keep it up if you want to keep people engaged.

Stuff not to do:

- Don't automate too much stuff. Tools like TweetDeck can save you time and effort, but you can often tell when something is scheduled. If you do use scheduling, make sure you have the ability to turn it off, quickly, as we mentioned earlier. Also, turn stuff off at Christmas – and any other holidays that might be appropriate for your organisation. Few things annoy us more on Christmas Day than tuning in to Twitter and seeing adverts for business products and services.

- Don't auto **DM** anyone through Twitter when they follow you. It's annoying.

- It's fine to share the same thing across different social media channels, although it might need some tailoring. But try not to do it at the same time. If someone is following you in more than once social space, they don't want to see the same content from you multiple times, all at once. You run the risk that they will disengage with you in one of those places.

Blogs and Blogging

We feel that this area is so important to leaders that we have given it its own chapter.

There are several different platforms on which you can set up a blog. Probably the most common is WordPress, and it is very user friendly. You don't need any specialist design skills to get one up and running and they have a help function if you get stuck. The key to a blog is that it is different to the usual formal corporate messaging stuff you will find on most company websites. It is personal, very much less formal and ideally, regular. It is about providing your unique insight to those that read it.

First things first. Why would you blog?

We are BIG advocates of blogging. It makes you think. It makes you creative. It improves your communication skills. But above anything, it is great for your personal brand.

It is our number one recommendation to aspiring social leaders. Blogging makes you real. Authentic. Accessible. It helps to build trust with the people that work for you. It provides a platform for feedback. A place to share your ideas and to gain input. It allows you to tell your own story. It can help to establish you as a thought leader. It can be read by employees or customers alike.

We could go on....

The downside is that it takes a little time to get the posts written, but they don't have to be long. Heck, if Richard Branson can do it, you can.

There are some practical things to think about when blogging. Although there are free sites out there, some, like WordPress, have paid for features. For example, you can pay to have your own domain name (otherwise, you will have something like thenameofyourblog@wordpress.com. Instead, you can have thenameofyourblog.com. It is a small difference but does look a bit more professional.

Also on WordPress, some visitors to your site will get adverts at the bottom of your posts. You can pay an annual fee to have an advert free site. Both cost relatively little. You can also pay for better graphics and layouts, but this is a personal choice and style thing. We recommend WordPress and we recommend paying for the no adverts option. It currently costs around £30 per year and it's better to spend that than find yourself with dodgy adverts on your professional site.

Our top tips on blogging for leaders:

1. Write it yourself. As we have said already (several times), this is *your* voice. The marketing team can do the corporate stuff

2. Stay regular. Ideally you should be looking at posting weekly, twice a month minimum

3. Stay away from controversial topics unless they are directly relevant to your business. Your employees probably do not need to know your opinion on the latest political issues for example. That said, making your writing current is a good thing

4. Don't be afraid to make them public. One of us worked at an organisation where the leader blogged… but then emailed it to everyone. It is better than nothing, true, but the real benefits from social media mean putting it out there for everyone to read (and even if you try to make it private, it can – and will – still get out there)

5. Don't ramble. A good blog post is around 400 words and makes one clear point or has one central message

6. Include images (your own or free ones – don't get caught with a copyright issue!)

7. Don't be afraid to include some personal stuff in your writing

Return on Investment

Ah yes, the elusive ROI. Proof that your efforts are working and delivering a desired outcome.

There is something of a leap of faith about being a social leader. Anything a little bit new always is. It is hard to put a value on how your employees will feel about you connecting directly with them and what the benefits will be. It is hard to put a value on a relationship and a connection. You can measure success to a point by looking at blog views, comments, likes and shares – essentially identifying how many people have engaged with your stuff. You can measure, too, any traffic to your corporate website via your social media activity, if that is part of the plan.

On the employee side, you can monitor and measure engagement levels – both via the traditional survey percentage type stuff or simply the level of activity that is taking place.

On the sales and marketing side there are measures there too. Sites like TweetReach can tell you how far your tweet travelled. Twitter itself now has an analytics function you can see for your own profile. You can measure follower numbers and track overall growth, whatever platform you are on. You can track leads from social feeds.

There are specific tools that you can use that will do some measurement on your behalf. Some are free and some are paid or **freemium**. As with most things, you will get a little more with the paid for versions or upgrades in terms of functionality.

The problem is that when it comes to measurement, you can focus a little too much on how many likes a post got, or the favourites, comments and retweets. Again, this tells you something, but not everything. Quality over quantity, any day of the week. Our advice is simple: if you are really worried about quantifiable proof, about precise measurement of success, then maybe go back to your investment spreadsheets. Because that is what social isn't all about.

For now, especially when you are starting out, we say don't worry about it too much. On the corporate side, yes. Measure your efforts to tailor your activity accordingly. But as a leader, just focus on being there. Learning the skills. Engaging and talking. Social style.

#Facepalm – how to avoid getting it wrong

There are horror stories everywhere about social media. You may have heard about the girl who befriended her boss on Facebook, and then complained about the tasks she was doing and described that same manager in her status as 'pervy'. He dismissed her via the comments section. Then there was the example of the employee who, before getting on a long-haul flight for a business trip to Africa, made a highly inappropriate comment on Twitter about AIDS and race. The tweet went viral, and the hashtag #hasjustinelandedyet was trending worldwide. Her employers had issued a statement confirming her dismissal before the plane touched down and her career has never recovered. Only recently an employee in the US was fired before even starting her new job, having posted a status update complaining about the job and the company in colourful language.

So here are some thoughts from us, on not making a leadership social media fail.

1. Don't try and be on every platform all the time. You couldn't do all of them well even if you tried and even if you employed a huge team whose sole job was just to do it. It's far better to target specific sites that work for you. For most organisations, that's Facebook and Twitter. However, one local artisan bakery we know of makes extensive use of Instagram – filling their followers' timelines with frankly irresistible images of fresh cakes and bread that can drive you crazy… Just decide and then tell your people where they can find you.

2. Train the people who work for you so that they are best placed to engage with you in this space. A little help plus a great role model can go a long way. Oh, and if you need any help with the training side of things, one of us just happens to do this for a living. #justsaying.

3. Don't buy followers or likes. It is obvious to anyone who understands social media and makes you look like you don't know what you are doing. If your content is interesting enough, you will get real ones, even if it takes a bit of time. If you try to short circuit the system, you're just missing the point.

4. Things we (and pretty much everyone else too) really hate: automated Direct Messages on Twitter – they do not, repeat *not*, engage anyone. Facebook pages that are never updated, or worse still are updated with meaningless corporate nonsense every 5 minutes. Blank LinkedIn connection requests that don't say why the person wants to link in with you. And when you accept one, an immediate email suggesting you buy their products. Try not to do any of these things.

5. Oversharing your own stuff. It is the equivalent of running around shouting 'I am awesome' in a very loud voice at everyone. Social media is not a one-way broadcast channel so you shouldn't treat it like one. Share other people's stuff, be useful, be chatty. People on social media respond to seeing others showing a bit of character rather than just issuing bland corporate statements all the time.

6. Being a social leader isn't about selling your products or promoting your brand. Don't ram this stuff down people's throats. This is about you. They will just unfollow you or disconnect with you. Be instead, a useful social human. Get it right and business might just be an outcome.

As a general rule, behave like you would in real life (and if you are not a very nice person in real life, then try harder!). If a customer came into your shop with a complaint, you would attend to them and try to resolve it as quickly and as peacefully as possible. If you met someone at a networking event, you wouldn't immediately start lecturing them about how wonderful your product was at the handshake. If someone talks to you, then usually you will talk back and establish a frame of reference and how you might be of mutual benefit.

Dealing with social media fails

It might happen. It is easy to make a mistake on social. Some of the biggest brands have done it. You might even find you do it yourself one day unintentionally. Do a Google search of 'biggest social media fails of' and pick a date of your choice. There are always a few annual round-ups. Or just search the internet for "Ed Balls Day". You'll soon see why.

The most important thing you can do if you have had a social media fail, is deal with it and deal with it fast. This often means issuing an apology. (In the case of "Ed Balls Day", by the way, the unfortunate Mr Balls has since embraced his mistake – which to be fair caused no harm to anyone except his personal pride – and now joins in with the annual mickey-taking that occurs).

If we are talking about your organisation's corporate social media account, you may or may not want to delete the offending item. If you have accidentally tweeted a link to a porn site, then you definitely do. If you have just said something a little insensitive, then you might want to leave it where it is and refer back to it – saying that you are sorry for its publication. Generally deleting a tweet or a status update won't get you very far anyway – you can pretty much guarantee that someone somewhere is going to have taken a screen shot.

If there is an opportunity to bring a little humour to the issue, then do so. It may be an idea to check your humour out first with someone else just in case – you probably don't need us to tell you that different people can have very different approaches to these matters. Most people will respect an 'ooops, we really made an arse of ourselves didn't we?'-type approach if the original social stuff wasn't offensive.

The second most important thing: in the words of The Hitchhiker's Guide to the Galaxy, DON'T PANIC. This stuff is very rare. You probably won't have to deal with it. You can do much to prevent yourself committing a major faux pas in the first place by understanding how it works, following our rules and – for others – having clear guidelines and providing training. But even if it does happen it is manageable.

Of course, it's not just yours or your corporate accounts that might end up with a fail situation you have to do something about. You might have an employee who does something totally inappropriate on their personal account. HR people are often brought up to believe that this is more common than it really is, in our opinion. Most people do have a degree of common sense about what is and is not acceptable. That said, your business should have a policy that sets out how it deals with potential disciplinary matters – make sure you follow it. If it is a relatively minor issue, then you might simply need to deal with the employee and issue some general reminders or training to other employees about what you consider acceptable – or not. If you end up with the situation where such a fail gets widely seen or shared, or you are getting formal complaints as an organisation, you must decide – do you stand by the employee or disassociate yourself from them? A timely 'this does not represent the views of the organisation' statement / tweet / status update etc., may be required. Just make sure that it does not prejudice any internal procedure that you will also need to follow.

Talk to your HR person, or seek external advice if necessary. Or message one of us if you get stuck.

Giving it a Go

We hope that our book has inspired you to get a little social, or encourage your organisation to do the same. When it comes to getting stuck in for yourself, we have three simple recommendations that we make to everyone getting social.

- Be You

- Dive In

- Share Stuff

Be You. On social media, just be yourself (unless of course you are a total arse, in which case, be nicer). Be authentic. People will know if you are not. Be open and honest to people. We have often met people first in a social world, and then gone on to meet them **IRL** (in real life). We have learnt one important thing; face to face, people are often very much like they are in the virtual world. If people do nothing but blatant self-promotion on Twitter, they are usually just like that at a networking event.

Dive In. There are plenty of people who just watch on Twitter. 'Lurking' is the official term. That is fine. But you will get the most out of it by getting involved and actively participating. People often complain, 'but I don't know what to say'. Our answer is simple a tweet has a shelf life of maybe 30 minutes' max, so just go for it. If you say something daft, chances are only a few people will notice it anyway. Just be brave (and exercise some common sense). Don't worry about crafting something profound. Tweet like no one is watching (apart from your mother).

Share Stuff. Everything like someone who shares their stuff. It is the best way to make new connections. People also like to follow people or connect with people who find interesting articles and pass them on through their networks. There are however plenty of folk around who just share their own stuff and nothing else. The minute you accept their LinkedIn connection they start sending you spam about why you should do business with them. You may want to avoid these people.

This is where we normally leave it when it comes to recommendations. But as this is about social *leadership*, we are going to make one more. **Be**

brave. This might be new to you. It might feel unusual. It might feel like you are opening yourself up. It might feel like taking a risk. But be brave, dare to fail. The potential opportunities are worth it.

JFDI, as one of us is fond of saying.

Finding stuff to share

It's not just about you.

As we have said elsewhere in this book, one of the big barriers to getting social in the early days for many people is knowing what to share.

What you definitely don't want to do is constantly share your own stuff. Firstly, it makes you look a bit like you are very impressed with yourself. And secondly, sharing other people's stuff is a great way to make contacts and expand your network. Everyone loves someone who shares their stuff. For the social leader, sharing content that interests you will make you a useful human. It will help the people that follow you learn along the way too, as well as make you a role model for good social practice.

Some practical ideas for finding stuff to share:

- Check out Ted talks on their website (http://www.ted.com/talks) and follow their feeds. There are Ted talks on almost everything, so there is bound to be something that interests you and is relevant to your organisation and followers.

- Follow the big sites like Harvard Business Review, Forbes, Inc and the Fast Company. They share a wide range of business content. You'll find a little **clickbait** too, but you will get information on current issues.

- Follow interesting people on whatever platform you go with. Share the stuff that you like and find interesting.

- Download an app called 'Pocket'. If you see something you like, you can just save it to Pocket and go back to it later.

- Fill in the minutes. The beauty of social media is that you don't need to spend hours on it. Standing in the queue to buy a coffee? Waiting for a meeting to start? Have yourself a little scroll through your social feeds. It is amazing what information you can get from just a few moments.

- Use the "lists" function on Twitter (on the desktop site, you can find this by clicking on your small profile picture on the "Home" tab and selecting "Lists"). This enables you to edit your timeline so that you have an alternate version where you only see posts from the people you have put in the list. This means you could make yourself some lists following just the stuff that you like to read and share to make it more time efficient.

- Still on Twitter, there is a "Moments" tab that tells you the latest news. There is also an area that tells you what is **trending** – you can change this to worldwide or local trends. If a subject that is of interest or relevance to you or your business is trending, it may indicate that it's a good time for you to search the hashtag or publish something of your own using that hashtag.

- Many business writers publish their articles on LinkedIn and given its professional focus, it can be a great place to find relevant content for your areas of interest. Beware of the quality though as many, despite high share counts, are clickbait.

Social Media That Rocks

Still stuck for ideas after all this stuff? Then check out some of the best social leaders out there (in our opinion anyway) and see what they are doing.

We will start with three of the biggest business guns.

Richard Branson - @richardbranson

One of the best out there. He tweets, blogs and writes over at LinkedIn. He allegedly does all his own stuff. He is out there regularly. Engages with others. A true social leadership role model. One of the things we like is how shareable his stuff is. He uses images and quotes, and some of his pieces are short and easy to read, making one clear point - one of our top blogging tips. He includes personal and family stuff too – so you really get a feeling for who he is and what he believes from his social stuff. Follow him and check out his activity.

Lynda Gratton - @lyndagratton

Professor and London Business School. Founder of the Hot Spots Movement which is all about the future of work. Author of great books. We consider Lynda to be a social leader because she engages and shares. Although not the most prolific of tweeters, she uses video and pictures, shares from events she is attending and doesn't just broadcast her own stuff. A highly professional example of social leadership.

Mark Zuckerberg

Given that he is Mr Facebook, it would be hard to see him as anything but a social leader. Not on Twitter, unsurprisingly, hence him not having a handle here. But you will of course find him all over his own platform.

Below is a list of other frequently recommended "big gun" leaders using social. Some of them are mainly in "broadcast" mode, some of them are genuinely engaging. For some reason, they are all American. Who you choose to follow is a very personal decision – and don't forget you can unfollow someone with the click of a button if they aren't working out for you – but this list gives you somewhere to start! As is so often the case in life, you'll probably learn just as much about how you want to use social media from someone who does it badly as from someone who does it brilliantly!

- Tim Cook (CEO, Apple) - @timcook

- Bill Gates (former CEO Microsoft) - @billgates

- Elon Musk (CEO, Tesla) - @elonmusk

- Marissa Mayer (CEO, Yahoo) - @marissamayer

- Martha Stewart (Entrepreneur) - @marthastewart

Your sector or areas of interest will undoubtedly have its own particular big guns – every sector does. From our own (largely HR and related) networks, here are a few examples of people that we think are doing a great job of being social leaders, in no particular order.

Steve Browne - @SBrowneHR

Steve is an Executive Director within HR. However, that isn't why we have chosen to feature him here. Instead, we have included him in this because he embodies what social leadership is all about. Generous sharing of a wide range of content, engaging with others within his professional community, supporting and championing others, blogging his own ideas about HR. A great example of how to do this social stuff whether you work in HR or not.

Tom Riordan - @tomriordan

Not an HR person but someone that we know a little bit. Tom is the CEO of Leeds City Council. He uses his Twitter feed to champion his city, his colleagues and the work that the council does. He isn't afraid of being real, including family stuff in there too. A great example of how to do Twitter if you lead an organisation.

Peter Cheese - @Cheese_Peter

Ok, he is the leader of the UK's professional HR body. But we are not sucking up. Much. We like Peter's tweets because he engages directly with the people that both work for him and are members of the professional body that he leads. He shares content not just from his own organisation but from other sources. He isn't afraid to do a little public social recognition and often engages directly with people who tweet him.

Phil Jones MBE - @philjones40

Phil is the (award-winning) Managing Director of Brother UK. He pops up regularly in our feeds with lots of good things to say about leadership, organisational development and business in general (note from Tim - plus he has great taste in music). He also shares lots of relevant business content, coupled with personal views, thoughts and music recommendations. A great example of a social business leader.

Jo Swinson - @joswinson

You may know of Jo as a politician who was a Minister in the Department for Business, Innovation and Skills (BIS) and Minister for Women from 2012 to 2015. Having left political office, she founded Equal Power Consulting and continued her work on equality and diversity issues. She is very active and engaging on Twitter – in the face of some occasionally challenging interaction from other users – and also shares personal thoughts and information too.

Asif Choudry - @AsifChoudry

Asif is Sales and Marketing Director at Resource. We know him through his amazing series of #CommsHero events (check out the hashtag on Twitter) at which he seamlessly links an excellent social media presence with pre-event collateral, the activities "in the room" and post-event follow up. He tweets and blogs enthusiastically, covering all aspects of his business and personal life. Also well-known for his love of Krispy Kreme doughnuts and Liverpool FC.

Rebecca Jeffery - @_rebeccajeffery

We have to confess that neither of us are avid watchers of the BBC's The Apprentice but we met 2016 contestant Becs IRL at a #CommsHero event (see above!) and had to find out more. We were really impressed with how she has incorporated social into her business and love her fresh, honest and natural approach to running her own account. Expect lots of pictures (especially selfies), working out loud and hashtags.

Dean Royles - @NHS_Dean

Director of HR and OD at Leeds Teaching Hospitals NHS trust. He blogs, tweets and podcasts as well as doing all that IRL stuff like speaking at conferences. It isn't all about numbers when it comes to social media, but he has a healthy 12K+ followers. He shares stuff from his own organisation, and is an advocate of social media in organisations and the NHS in particular. We like him.

Kate Griffiths-Lambeth - @KateGL

We've included Kate in this list because not only is she generally a great example of social leadership, but because of something quite special she has been doing for the last three years. In December, and usually on into January, Kate curates the Advent Blog series. Every day, there is a new blog from a different writer, all focusing on an annual theme. Kate thoughtfully curates each one with personal words and reflections. It is a real labour of love, but a daily treat for the reader. This embodies social leadership for us. Sharing. Encouraging others. Providing a space. This is part of the joy of Twitter for us. You can find all the blog posts by using the hashtag #AdventBlogs. We very much recommend that you do.

Simon Blake - @simonablake

Simon is Chief Executive of the National Union of Students and a fantastic example of how a CEO can use social media to communicate with and engage a wide variety of stakeholders. Simon uses Twitter brilliantly to keep his followers informed, not just of what he and the NUS are up to, but also on other projects in which he is involved. He often uses social media to recognise colleagues' work and post pictures of his beautiful dog, Dolly. What more could you ask for in a social leader?

Of course, there is much more to social leadership than being the person who is at or near the top of an organisation. Because of the very nature of social, people can become influential – let's go as far as saying they are social leaders – by virtue of what they share and write. Social leaders may write themselves and share their expertise. They may campaign for good causes. Go above and beyond for their profession. Are really very smart. Or occasionally, just make us laugh.

So it's always worth remembering that to be a social leader, you don't necessarily have to have the CEO title. Dare we use the rather hideous phrase 'thought leader'? I think we just have. Sorry about that.

Final Thoughts (Almost)

We said at the start of the book that this is the social world, and it is true. This is the new normal. Social media guru Erik Qualman, who we have mentioned elsewhere in this book, says something that goes along the lines of "we no longer have a choice whether we do social media, just how well we do it". This is very true for all businesses, large and small.

Social has already had an impact on how we work, but we are only just starting to realise its full potential. The ways in which we have worked for decades will be impacted. Frankly, social blows the bloody doors off.

The truth is – we must adapt.

Because we know what happens to the organisations, functions, professions and leaders that can't, don't, or simply won't. We have all seen the case studies, the corporate corpses stinking up the joint. Even very large companies, with plenty of people paid lots of money who should have seen this stuff coming have been taken by surprise and have paid the price. Therefore, the business leader must be even more ready to spot change coming and adapt accordingly.

So, to leaders who say that theirs is "not that sort of business", that they don't have those sort of customers, that they don't see that it is relevant to them, we say simply this:

Early adopter or laggard, organisations cannot put their collective heads in the sand and pretend it's not happening. Social cannot be constrained through policy and procedure, and neither can organisations afford to try to fit old solutions to these new challenges. You can't stop it or ignore it but you can embrace it and seize the opportunities.

Let us give you an example. You may well have heard of Uber. They are the taxi company operating in several cities across the UK now. You download an app and when you want a cab, instead of heading down to the taxi rank and standing in a queue in the cold, or attempting to wave one down in the street, you tell the app where you are and where you want to go, and a taxi will soon arrive. Technology putting the consumer and the seller together. It sounds like a great idea. Only some people didn't think so – namely the black cab company in London. They chose to fight Uber. To take them to court and try and prevent them operating by focusing on technicalities. They didn't win. We would suggest that they would have been better spending time understanding how their world has changed, and how they could respond. You can't fight the future.

We meet people all the time who don't get social, don't like social and don't think it is relevant to them or their career or their business. They think it's just some fad that will go away. Or they tell us that they keep meaning to give it a go, in a voice that implies no interest or intent at all. We offer them these challenges:

Does a black and white television set still take up space in your living room?

Do you long for your original, big, old Nokia mobile phone, so you can play just one more game of "Snake"?

Do you lament the lost days of the manual typewriter and the carbon copy paper?

Do you still get good value from your fax machine?

Of course not. Because the world moved on and we moved with it. And now it is time to move again.

This is the social world. It demands social leaders. Are you ready?

Tools and Techniques

Here's some useful stuff to know more about, in no particular order. That might just make things easier or more manageable.

Hootsuite

This is a platform that can help you organise your social media accounts. To be honest, we'd suggest that this is somewhere you might want to think about going once you are really up to speed with using social.

Lists

We mentioned this earlier, but it bears repeating. A useful way to organise your Twitter timeline is a list. This simply means that you create lists of people and accounts, in order to organise or categorise. This means that when you want to catch up, you don't have to check back through a busy timeline, but can just select a few key areas. For example, Gemma has a 'favetweeps' list, so that she can quickly check what her Twitter friends have been up to.

Lists can either be private for your eyes only or public for the benefit of other users to see who else it might be worth following.

Scheduling Tweets

This is a way that you can schedule tweets to be sent, even when you are not around to do it yourself. There are specialist apps to do this, like Hootsuite or TweetBeam among others. You write the tweets, then pick the time and dates that you want them to go out. It is a good way to keep your presence up, perhaps when you are on holiday for example. Also, in a global world you can get a 24/7 reach – social media is the conversation that never sleeps! Some people that we follow set their previous blogs to tweet every couple of weeks. For example..... *'One from my blog archive.....'* This has the benefit of making your written content useful for a long time.

Just be careful about it. For example, if there was to be a serious incident or national disaster, turn them off, quickly. Also, don't schedule tweets at times when no-one wants to talk business, like Christmas Day.

Selfie

The art of taking a picture of yourself. Can be taken by hand or the popular-with-tourists selfie stick. Capable of being shared on most platforms but especially on sites like Instagram, Snapchat and Facebook. A great addition to the "this is what I'm doing right now" kind of post. Popular with a whole host of celebs. Check out the Kardashians. If you must.

Using Hashtags

We find that people get very #confused about hashtags. First of all, don't overuse them – unless you're tweeting from an event for example, at which you'll want to ensure the hashtag is in every tweet or message so they can be found by people who don't necessarily follow you. Second, you can just make one up. Maybe you're at a #henparty. Or a #productgiveaway. Or maybe it's time for a #FridayFunny. You can search for existing hashtags in the search area of Twitter. The easiest thing to do is research them or simply see what others are using. We will probably have one for this very book. #SocialLeaders maybe?

A Social Media and Technology Glossary

App

An app (short for "application") is to your mobile device as a programme is to your computer (although the word "app" is creeping into computing now too). It's the specific software that allows you to do – well, anything. Hence the phrase originally coined by Apple that "there's an app for that". There almost always is.

Blog/Blogging

A blog (the word is an abbreviation of the word "weblog") is essentially text that an author has published online. Blogs are usually informal and cover a topic of personal interest: from leadership to fitness, fashion to music. People blog about their mental health, their politics, their favourite recipes. There are sites like **Tumblr** that allow you to blog directly into their format, or you can use something like **WordPress** which allows you to build your own website around your blogging.

Clickbait

Slang term for when the title of an article or blog is cunningly designed to pique the reader's curiosity and make them want to click on it to find out more. For example, "This woman slipped in the street and what happened next will amaze you". It can also be used to describe when an author has used specific popular jargon words aimed at encouraging more people to read their article. If your article is described as click bait, you can assume the describer is not intending it as a compliment...

Cloud computing

When we think of storing computer data, most of us think of the separate PC boxes we have under or on our desks which are linked together by our office network and the internet. Cloud computing is storing data on big servers remotely rather than on the individual boxes. One of the main benefits is that it can be accessed by anyone with an internet connection anywhere. If you've ever used Dropbox or Microsoft's OneDrive, you've used cloud computing.

Coffice

Slang term. Increasingly commonly in our knowledge-based economy, some types of workers aren't based in a typical office environment but are usually out and about and therefore hold meetings (or just hog the Wi-Fi) in coffee shops all over the country and generally treating public establishments as their office. So coffee shop + office = coffice.

Cognitive Assistant

The Cognitive Assistant is the next phase of development of what we used to call Artificial Intelligence (or AI) – it allows you to interact directly, usually verbally, with your technology. If you use an iPhone or iPad and have ever experienced the joy of Siri, you've used a Cognitive Assistant. Google offers Google Assistant to do a similar job. One of the benefits of using a mobile device is the use of GPS – ie they know where you are. So you can effectively treat them like personal assistants – so you could say for example "Next time I'm in the office, remind me to water the plants". Through Siri/Google Assistant your device will recognise when you are next in the location you have told it is your office and will do exactly that. Scary, eh? Amazon are now marketing the Echo as a similar system based in a smart Bluetooth speaker.

Content

In the context of the internet, content is literally anything that is produced and can then be shared: articles, blogs, photos, videos, presentation slide decks... you name it. The idea behind content creation is that you can share it across multiple platforms a number of times to ensure that everyone who follows you (and preferably lots of people who don't and then want to) gets to see it.

Converged devices

Remember when your mobile phone just made phone calls and that was about it? Current smartphones are so much more than just phones and can do all sorts of things with data, geo-location and other (sometimes slightly scary) technology. Mobile telephony and data – which were once chalk and cheese – have converged into one device: hence converged devices.

Crowdsourced/crowdsourcing & crowdfunding

Have you ever posted a question online like "Can anyone recommend somewhere to eat in Liverpool city centre?" Then (assuming you got some answers) you have crowdsourced. It is basically getting answers or input from a wide range of people using your online networks. You can crowdsource just about anything. TripAdvisor is a good example of crowdsourced feedback – they don't employ anyone to go out and review hotels, restaurants or attractions, they simply provide the platform to collate and co-ordinate the feedback from thousands of "ordinary" people. This kind of open feedback model is a growing area online.

Likewise, there is a growth in using social technology to "crowdfund" projects, especially in the arts and music arenas. This flips the traditional music industry model - invest in album, make album, market album, hope it makes enough money to cover costs and turn a bit of profit – by getting the money needed to make the project happen first through asking fans to contribute. The fans usually get something in return – for example a signed copy or some other individualised merchandise that acknowledges their input. The same approach is being used to fund new products, often in the new technology market.

Visit www.kickstarter.com for more information and examples.

Enterprise Social Network/ESN

An ESN is basically just a private social network, usually restricted to one particular organisation. The big advantage of using an ESN rather than an existing network such as Twitter or Facebook is privacy: what is posted cannot be read by anyone outside of the company. This is obviously important in terms of intellectual property and competitive advantage. The most common platform is currently Microsoft's **Yammer** but everyone (well, everyone who is interested in this sort of thing) is waiting to see what the relatively new *"Workplace by Facebook"* will do to the market.

Facebook

https://www.facebook.com

The undisputed daddy of social media sites with so many users worldwide that if they all got together, they would form the most populous country in the world. Yes, bigger than China.

Freemium

Slang term. A common business model, particularly in selling **apps**, is to make the main product available for free but then to charge for certain features or additional content. It's a combination (or portmanteau if you're as pretentious as Tim) of "free" and "premium", in case you're wondering.

Glassdoor

http://www.glassdoor.co.uk

Best described as "TripAdvisor for companies", this international website allows employees and former employees to rate and review organisations they have worked for as employers. Anyone can start talking about a business – so if you employ people, someone else might just open your account for you.

Google+/G+

https://plus.google.com

Google+ is Google's attempt at a social network to compete with Facebook. It hasn't been as successful in terms of sheer numbers as Facebook but it does have some very cool features that we love – such as Google Hangouts which is a better version of Skype. It's underrated, arguably underused and there is regularly discussion about whether Google will "kill it off".

Hashtag/#

Popularised by Twitter – to the extent that Facebook had to recognise them too – the hashtag is basically a keyword that allows you to tag or "file" a tweet against a subject so that if you search for that particular term, you get a list of tweets which contain it, regardless of whether you follow those people. You can immediately see how using hashtags properly can extend the reach of your tweets as they won't necessarily just be seen by your followers.

Who comes up with hashtags? Well, anyone. You can start a hashtag if you want to – just stick the hash (or pound sign if you're American) in front of some text. There are some common ongoing hashtags such as #FF which stands for "Follow Friday" in which Twitter users suggest other users that people should follow. The trick is finding out which ones apply to you and/or your organisation. We use #HR and #hrblogs quite a lot. Sometimes events have their own hashtags so you know that tweets that contain them are from or inspired by that event.

The hashtag has become such a common part of the language on Twitter that regular users often use a hashtag in a jokey way, usually to finish off a tweet, such as "Just ended up in McDonalds for lunch #dietfail".

Instagram

https://instagram.com

Instagram is a social media site with photographs (and a bit of video), rather than status updates, at its heart. It is very straightforward as social media sites go (upload photo, say a little bit about it) but one of its most appealing factors is the ability to apply "filters" to your photos which can make them look pretty cool, if we do say so ourselves. It is entirely acceptable to post photos of your breakfast/lunch/dinner on Instagram and anyone who tells you otherwise is lying.

Internet of Things

This is one of those terms that has such massive reach and coverage that it could easily fill a book on its own. Basically, it is a general term used to describe the current move towards all sorts of devices being connected and operated through or via the internet.

The possibilities are endless and we are only just beginning to get our heads around them. Imagine your fridge knew what you'd just taken out of it and could add it automatically to your next online shopping order. That's something the internet of things would take care of. A heart monitor that keeps an eye on your dicky ticker and can identify - before you even feel it - that something untoward is happening and can notify both you and your local Accident & Emergency? The internet of things makes these kinds of things possible. The potential applications are mind blowing.

IRL/In Real Life

Slang term, most often found on Twitter, to describe meeting someone physically (i.e. In Real Life) rather than communicating online, as in "It was fab to meet @HR_Gem IRL today".

Klout

https://klout.com

Klout is primarily a tool that enables you to measure your impact on social media. It uses information gathered from your social media profiles (such as how many people have read your status, interacted with you or shared your content) to generate a score which enables you to see how you are "performing". We're a bit suspicious of it to be honest as it feels a bit too forced. Was popular a few years ago. Most people have now forgotten it exists.

LinkedIn

https://www.linkedin.com

Simply put, LinkedIn is "Facebook for professionals". It allows you to show off your career achievements and showcase yourself for the purpose of professional networking and/or seeking job opportunities. As we've said elsewhere in this book, we're not huge fans but we do feel we kind of have to have profiles and engage with it sometimes...

Personal Brand

You, essentially – or rather, how you are perceived. Often referred to as 'what people say about you when you are not in the room'.

Pinterest

https://www.pinterest.com

An online virtual noticeboard: a place for "pinning" images, videos and links onto your own noticeboards, which can be public or private. You will find everything on there from recipes, wedding ideas, fitness inspiration and motivational quotes.

Search Engine Optimisation (SEO)

Something of a dark art of the modern world, SEO is designing and coding websites in such a way that they appear higher up the list of results when internet users search for certain key words – and therefore ultimately drive more traffic to the site.

Slack

https://slack.com

Slack describes itself as "A messaging app for teams". We think of it as part old skool internet message-board, part social media app. It has a number of advantages over the traditional email "Reply All" project management approach and it isn't public in that you have to join a particular "team" to see all their content. Slack operates on a **freemium** basis so you can give it a try for nothing and if your organisation is small will probably be able to continue using it for nowt. We even know people who use Slack to organise their social lives and keep in touch with friends.

SlideShare

www.slideshare.net

A site that allows presenters to share slide decks with their audience and indeed anyone on the internet. A simple way to maximise your production of content if you have to give a presentation at any stage!

Snail mail

Slang term used to describe traditional postal services as opposed to almost-instantaneous electronic mail (as no-one calls email any more).

Snapchat

https://snapchat.com

A messaging app. Users can take pictures or videos and add text or drawings to them, then share them with their friends. The user decides how long the 'snaps' are available for – but it's usually just a few seconds. Clearly this limits its business application a little, but there are still brands out there making the most of it. It has quite a young user demographic – the **selfie** is a very popular on SnapChat.

Trending

A term used mostly in connection with Twitter. Refers to hashtags, terms or words that are the most popular at any given time. Trends can be shown as worldwide or local. To make a conference or product hashtag trend is the Holy Grail of all social media coverage activity.

Tumblr

https://www.tumblr.com

Pronounced "Tumbler" (in case you were wondering), this site is arguably the simplest way to host your own blog as it does all the hard work for you. You can upload text, images, video or quotes to your Tumblr blog and then share the link widely across other social networks. Ideal if you don't want to invest the time and energy into setting up a WordPress site or want to dip a toe into blogging.

Tweeps

Slang term used to describe followers on Twitter – comes from Twitter people/Twitter peeps/Tweeps. One of Gem's favourite words.

TweetDeck

https://tweetdeck.twitter.com

A good example of an app/website that helps you use Twitter in a more flexible way than Twitter's own app. For example, you can have a number of different panels open at once showing your timeline, notifications, any tweets featuring a particular hashtag etc. You can also use TweetDeck to schedule tweets so that they tweet at a particular time on a particular day. Which is very handy if you're going to be away at a key moment.

Twitter

https://twitter.com

In case you hadn't noticed through the rest of this book, Twitter is our favourite social networking site. Officially known as a "micro-blogging" site, users have 140 characters in which to make posts. Posts can include images and video (usually as links) or just be links to content elsewhere. You can find people discussing almost anything on Twitter at any time so whatever you're into, professional or personal, you'll find it going on somewhere on here too. Without Twitter, it's possible, indeed probable that we'd never have met and that would be a Very Bad Thing indeed.

Vlog

Not a Klingon word from Star Trek, honestly: a vlog is simply a blog in the medium of video rather than text. With the increasing availability of reasonable quality video recording – most smartphones now can achieve a suitable picture for uploading – some people choose to present their blog personally and upload it to YouTube. On the other hand, some people hear the sound of their own voice and scuttle immediately back to their keyboards.

Wearable technology

Fairly self-explanatory this one: if carrying a phone is too much effort for you, look forward to the much-hyped adoption of wearable tech. Google may have killed off Glass (the ones that looked like a pair of glasses) but the concept looks like it's here to stay as people get excited about their Apple watches. For now, they still need to be connected to smartphones but who knows how long that will last? Still regarded by many as the Next Big Thing.

WordPress

https://wordpress.com

This site allows you to build your own website or blog from scratch with a bare minimum of programming knowledge. If you want the flexibility of having your own website but don't want to spend years learning how to code, go here. There is plenty of help available in both the official help section and elsewhere on the internet so you shouldn't have too much trouble finding the answers to your set up questions. The results can be very impressive and the possibilities are pretty much endless.

Yammer

https://www.yammer.com

Probably the biggest private internal social media platform (or **ESN**) used by employers to facilitate and encourage sharing and collaboration across organisations. It plays nicely with the Microsoft Office packages we all know and sort-of love and in the right hands can transform how organisations work together.

YouTube

www.youtube.com

Fundamentally a video-sharing website, it has become one of the most visited search engines in the world, which goes to show how much we love our video. You can find everything that could possibly be filmed on here from inspirational speeches and talks (check out TED talks) to a guy in his garage explaining how to change your car's headlight bulb, clips of your favourite TV programmes, fan tributes to movies and lots of pets doing funny things.

And Finally: Getting Started on Twitter & LinkedIn

As we said at the start of this book, we recognise that for some people, social media is still a great unknown. We recognise that some people who buy this book won't have any presence on social at all yet. If this applies to you, then here is a very brief handy guide on how to set up accounts on LinkedIn and Twitter just to get you started, and a summary of the specific language used on each site.

For the rest of you who are already out there, feel free to get on with tweeting and sharing.

Twitter

Go to www.twitter.com and follow the sign up process. It is a straightforward process and Twitter will guide you through it.

As you go through signing up, Twitter will suggest a username for you (this is called your Twitter handle). For example, @TimScottHR.

You don't have to follow their suggestion, but do choose something simple and memorable, and ideally that links to your business. Some popular names will be taken, so you might have to get inventive! Make sure it is something you can live with for the long term, otherwise you might find yourself changing it on your marketing material. Try not to make your username too long, as it will use up characters when you are tweeting or people are tweeting you.

When you have set up your account, the next step is to find some people to follow. Twitter will give you some suggestions to begin with, but try searching for people that you know who are already tweeting, or even a few celebrities just to get you started. The more people you follow, the more accurate Twitter's recommendations for new people to follow will become.

Set up a 'bio'. This is clearly stating who you are, and gives people an idea about what you will tweet about so they can decide if they want to follow you or not. It's generally ok on Twitter to put in a little something personal too, within reason. Check out our bios for some ideas! You can also include a link here to your website, which will help generate traffic for you in that direction.

<u>Other stuff...</u>

- You might find it useful to download the Twitter app for your phone, so you can tweet or check your time line on the go.

- Keep your eye on the 'notification's tab at the top of the app or the Desktop. This is where it will show if someone tweets with your Twitter handle. It is good practice to reply to them or engage back, even it is just a simple tweet to say... *'Hey @TimScottHR, thanks for sharing my blog post!'*

- If you follow someone, and decide you don't enjoy their tweets, you can just unfollow them at any time. Just go into their profile and click 'unfollow'.

- You can amend your bio or profile at any time, along with your privacy settings, by just going into the settings menu (it looks like a cog wheel on the top right hand side of the page).

- If you see a tweet you like, you can 'favourite' it – and it will stay in your favourites list so you can return to it.

- Twitter allows you to make your tweets private, but this really isn't any good for an aspiring social leaders' account.

- Follow people from your industry and competitors. It will help you understand what others are tweeting about.

Once you are set up – all you need to do is send your first tweet – and we have given you plenty of rules on that already!

LinkedIn

Go to www.linkedin.co.uk and follow the sign-up process. You can do it via the app, but you might find it a little easier on a desktop – the user experience is generally better there. LinkedIn will guide you through the set-up process, so simply follow the steps, which is essentially all about setting up a personal profile to begin with.

This is all about you – your career history, your education and your skills. You can choose whether you make your profile publicly available or just to your connections. You can amend this at any time in the 'settings' tab.

You can also add a description about you and your skills and experience (the summary), links to your website, a list of your skills, education and qualifications and join relevant groups.

Other stuff…

- LinkedIn will recommend to you people that you might know based on the information you input into your profile. You will see this on the right-hand side of the page.

- Most companies have LinkedIn groups or pages. You can follow these for their updates.

- LinkedIn will highlight news and articles that might be of interest to you. These will appear at the top of the page.

- You can choose how much of your profile you make public, or just how much you show to the people you are connected with. Adjust this in your privacy settings.

- If you want to share content on LinkedIn, such as an article or blog post, you will find most online content has a 'share' button, or LinkedIn icon. Simply click, and up will pop a box for you to edit (you don't have to, but you can include a comment about it if you want) and then simply click the button to share the link with your network. Anything you share can be seen by any of your connections.

- As well as connecting with people on LinkedIn, you can follow people too. For example, you can follow business leaders or writers.

- You can also give recommendations to other people that you know or ask them to recommend you too.

Once your account is set up and your profile is complete, you can begin to connect with people. Start by searching for people that you already know. If you click onto their profile, you will see a button that allows you to send a connection request. On the desktop version, LinkedIn will ask you how you know the person. On the app, it just sends it. It is considered polite to personalise the request. For example: *"Hi Gem, we met at a networking event recently, it would be great to connect with you on LinkedIn"* is just fine.

There is one simple rule with LinkedIn. The more connections you have, the greater the reach of your profile and your brand messages. So get connecting!!

Other people will begin to connect with you too. You can see these, along with messages and updates from your network, in the top right hand corner (on the desktop version). You can choose whether to accept or ignore those connection requests.

There is just one more thing to note about LinkedIn. You will get lots of notifications and emails from them unless you organise this. For example, if you join a group, you will automatically get a daily email telling you about activity in that group. This might very quickly become annoying. You can however manage this in your settings area. You can set your notifications to suit your needs.

We now have just one final thing to say....

Good luck and enjoy!

Gemma and Tim